To Eileen
All our Love
Peg & Doug

Xmas/84

RACE FOR THE ROSE

Also by Charles Lynch

China, One-Fourth of the World
You Can't Print That!
Our Retiring Prime Minister

RACE FOR THE ROSE

ELECTION 1984

Charles Lynch

 METHUEN

Toronto   New York   London   Sydney   Auckland

Canadian Cataloguing in Publication Data

Lynch, Charles, 1919–
  Race for the rose

ISBN 0-458-98460-4

1. Turner, John N., 1929–   2. Liberal Party
of Canada.   3. Canada. Parliament – Elections,
1984.*   I. Title.

JL197.L5L96 1984   324.27106   C84-099439-7

Printed and bound in the United States of America

1 2 3 4 5   84   89 88 87 86 85

CONTENTS

PROLOGUE

As I prepare to leave the ship Gritanic,
To spend my twilight years in Montreal
I contemplate the future without panic
The universe has folded, after all.
But if I hand it to that bastard, Turner,
It won't be with a friendly fare-thee-well,
For I am beautiful,
But he has loved me never,
And so forever he can go to hell!
> Trudeau song, Parliamentary Press Gallery
> Dinner, April, 1984.

This is about the decline and fall of the Liberal Party of
Canada, and the three men who had most to do with the
political events of 1984—Pierre Trudeau, John Turner, and
Brian Mulroney.

It is about the longest election campaign in Canadian
history; one that started in 1979 with the defeat of Joe
Clark's Conservative government and the comeback of
Pierre Trudeau, to exhaust what remained of Liberal credibility.

The first four years of this five-year election campaign
were taken up with Liberal diversions and evasions, and
Conservative convulsions. The Tories hunted and hounded
Joe Clark until finally Brian Mulroney out-chinned and out-
elbowed him, assuming the party leadership and drawing a
bead on Trudeau.

Mulroney had a game plan and he followed it to the
letter, up to his killing of the Grits in the historic election of

1984, the end of an era as John Turner himself called it, and the end of the Liberal Party as we had known it for all our lives. In the final years, the symbol of power was the rose in Pierre Trudeau's lapel—and when he handed it to Turner, it was wilted, and Liberals were left to wonder if their overthrow of Joe Clark in 1979 had been such a good idea.

From the moment of Mulroney's 1983 convention win over Joe Clark, the sands began to shift under Trudeau's feet, and at one stage the Gallup Poll read Conservatives 63, Liberals 23. Trudeau launched an abortive global peace initiative that helped matters somewhat, but Mulroney's continued popularity convinced an increasing number of Grits that Trudeau had to go.

The clearer it became that a change was in the wind, the higher the Liberals climbed, to the point where a John Turner candidacy became more and more likely, the supposition being that Turner's interest was in the prime ministership, or nothing.

The man to beat was Mulroney, whose own popularity was slipping in the face of renewed interest in the Liberals. There was a momentary popularity blip in Mulroney's favour after Trudeau's retirement announcement on February 29, but then the polls gave a lurch and the Liberals surged ahead, raising the prospect that whoever won the leadership convention might win the election that had to follow.

So every Grit drew a bead on Mulroney, and the Conservative leader bided his time, conceding the media convention hype to the Liberals, and travelling up and down the land letting people have a look at him.

Everywhere in Canada, Conservative nomination meetings were drawing record crowds, including more than 4,000 voting delegates to the Ottawa Civic Centre, 500 more than would come to the Liberal leadership convention. That was to nominate a Tory candidate in the Nepean-Carleton by-election to succeed the late, much loved Walter Baker.

Even in Quebec, Conservative nominating meetings

were drawing huge crowds, causing Mulroney to crack that Tory meetings were drawing more six-year-olds than the Liberals were getting adults.

The Liberals had the hoopla edge—the widespread coverage of Trudeau's retirement, the leadership campaign, the convention, the Turner takeover. Not until the election was called would Brian Mulroney get an even break and be able to make his own race for the rose. Meantime he could be grateful for all the plugs the Grits were giving him, including the crack that the man the Liberals chose was a more polished, more accomplished, more experienced Mulroney. Liberals were left to ponder leadership candidate John Roberts' repeated warning that if given a choice between a real Conservative and a Liberal imitation, they were likely to vote for the real thing.

Then there was the suspicion that Pierre Trudeau thought more highly of Mulroney than he did of Turner, of Jean Chrétien, or of any of the Liberal candidates. And Quebec Liberal Leader Robert Bourassa seemed happy to have his provincial troops work for Mulroney federally. Jean Chrétien said he would put a stop to all that, if elected leader, which he wasn't.

1

THE RETURN OF THE RATCHET KID

Hammy, baby.

"He calls me 'Hammy, baby'!"

The speaker was G. Hamilton Southam, the patrician member of the publishing clan, former diplomat, and patron of the arts who once shamed a reluctant Liberal government into building the $50-million National Arts Centre in Ottawa, though he didn't disclose the price tag until the job was done.

G. Hamilton Southam was pouting about his one-time Rockcliffe neighbour, John Turner, and he was wondering what kind of man would call him "Hammy, baby," and whether such a man would make a sound prime minister.

"But sir," said I, with the respect all Southam people use toward all Southams, "he calls everybody baby. Sometimes even sweetheart, or fella, or guy." I suggested these terms mightn't be a true measure of Turner's mind, since he probably didn't even hear himself saying them.

"It's like the way he used to talk about the broads," I went on. "Just a way of speaking, like the way Dief used to whinny, or Trudeau using cuss words, or Joe Clark saying 'specificity'."

"Look," I added, "Turner is a throwback to the fifties, or the forties, in his reflexes. Think of The Fonz, with class. Imagine him in the jock fraternity at the University of British Columbia, calling himself 'Chick' and using it as a byline as a sports reporter, because it seemed snappy. He talked jive—to one of the campus studs he'd say, 'who ya featurin' tonight, baby?'''

Hammy baby sniffed and changed the subject before I could interject that John Arena, the proprietor of Winston's watering hole in Toronto and scorekeeper of the elite, said of Turner that ''one always recognizes breeding, and John Turner has it.''

Sounds like something out of *The Right Stuff*, which turned out to be a Grade B movie, and killed astronaut John Glenn's political ambition. Somebody else described Turner as a combination of the Duke of Edinburgh and Sammy Glick.

I recalled Turner, as minister of finance, saying the way to tackle inflation was not to try to do it all at once.

''We have to ratchet it down gradually,'' he said.

''Did you say rat shit?'' we inquired, thinking that the economy was turning that way, though it seemed unusual for a minister of finance to admit it.

''Ratchet!'' Turner replied. ''Ratchet it down.''

It didn't work, any more than Trudeau's famous wrestling inflation to the ground had worked. Nothing Turner tried seemed to work, which put him in the sad tradition of all Canadian finance ministers, so he quit and sought his own answer to inflation amid the greenbacks of Bay Street, with never a backward glance, pitching his seat over to the Tories with a mixture of spite and satisfaction. There was even talk of his crossing the floor and seeking the Conservative leadership, which was coming vacant as a result of Robert Stanfield's reluctance to face Pierre Trudeau for a fourth time, when he would have cleaned Trudeau's clock.

That was in 1975, and for the better part of ten years Turner lay in the political weeds, his gills barely twitching, saying nothing newsworthy, doing nothing newsworthy and, so far as the public was concerned, thinking no newsworthy thoughts.

He developed the boardroom look that comes from expensive food, expensive facials, expensive clothes, and the mandatory whiteness of hair—if Trudeau was Marlon Brando playing Napoleon, Turner was Robert Young or Charlton Heston, miscast as chairman of the board.

Yet segments of the media, like Pavlov's dog, salivated at the mention of his name—a name, notably, that never passed the lips of Pierre Trudeau, who soldiered on, aided by the likes of "Thumper" Don Macdonald, Marc Lalonde, Allan MacEachen and Jean Chrétien. As the years passed, the legend grew that he had been a great minister of justice, and a great finance minister, and people too young to remember came to believe it.

There were casualties galore on the political battlefield while Turner was absent without leave (any leave, that is, but his own).

Down went Robert Stanfield, his hopes dashed in Turner's last election, when old Blue Eyes stole Stanfield's best stuff (notably the indexing of tax benefits), but crapped all over the Tory leader's sombre call for wage-and-price controls.

Joe Clark came and went, and still Turner turned his back, bypassing a run for the Liberal leadership when Trudeau staged his First Going in 1979. Turner opted out, saying he had to feed his wife and kids.

Brian Mulroney emerged, and still there was no sign or sound of Turner. Except in Media—the press, the radio, the television. Through the years, they kept his name alive as a future leader, bestowing on him that most precious and elusive political quality, recognition.

What we saw was a genuine Canadian contribution to the democratic process, the notion that the way to political success is to stay out of politics. Richard Nixon had demonstrated the principle in the United States between 1960 and his great triumph in 1968, when he amassed a fortune in Wall Street. But at least, in those intervening years, Nixon had dabbled in politics and taken at least a passing interest in the affairs of the Republican Party, wallowing, as it was, in the wilderness of opposition. Turner, from Bay Street, held himself aloof, even though his former party was in power for almost the whole of his exile.

The idea of triumph by abstention seems as Canadian as

Trivial Pursuit, the snowmobile, or that greatest of all Canadian inventions, the federal-provincial conference, where leaders meet with the sole purpose of agreeing to do nothing.

The principle of getting to the top in Canadian politics by staying out is an extension of the earlier Canadian thesis that if you avoid military service in wartime, you get to become prime minister after. Witness William Lyon Mackenzie King, who busied himself with labour problems in the United States during the First World War, or Pierre Trudeau, who concentrated on his own concerns during the Second.

Trudeau combined the two techniques, avoidance of war and abstention from politics, by becoming prime minister only three years after joining the Liberal Party for which, until the moment of his belated conversion, he had expressed nothing but contempt, preferring the socialist CCF and its successor, the NDP.

Joe Clark became leader of the Tories on no stronger a recommendation than his four years as an obscure backbench member of parliament.

And Brian Mulroney had never held elected office of any kind when he displaced Clark in 1983, and had never run for anything apart from national party leadership. He was, however, the first national party leader ever to have been president of a major industrial corporation, the Iron Ore Company of Canada.

So it was that John Turner's political career languished during his years in the early Trudeau cabinets, but it flourished when he went to Toronto to make money. He achieved more from his seat at Winston's than he ever did from his seat in the House of Commons.

Politicians came and went without gaining a mention.

Some, like Clark, were mocked for doing their best, or pilloried for having no chin or walking funny.

Down went the doughty charmer, Jean-Luc Pepin.

Francis Fox disgraced himself.

Into obscurity went Barney Danson, Judd Buchanan, Tony Abbott, Don Jamieson, Gérard Pelletier, Jean Marchand.

In Quebec, Claude Ryan flared up and spluttered out, a pope defrocked.

Turner kept being put on the lists of post-Trudeau prospects for leadership, and usually his name led all the rest.

So when it came time for Trudeau to admit he was licked—or, more correctly, that he would be if he ran again—there was Turner, all slicked up with someplace to go, a fat file of press clippings as his credentials—press clippings containing nothing of substance, but with the name spelled right. TURner in English, TurNER in French. Neat.

And when Turner announced his availability, after Trudeau's walk in the blizzard, the media presented the Liberal Party with its new leader and the country with its new prime minister, sight unseen.

The hailing of Turner's advent was so extreme, and so complete, it very nearly broke Jean Chrétien's heart, because it seemed so unreasonable, and so unfair. It's true that all's fair in politics, and Trudeau had preached "reason before passion," but what was this?

Had somebody bought up all the space on Turner's behalf?

What had the man said, or done, to merit such blanket coverage, such adulation from the usually cynical scribes and garglers of media?

Nothing, Chrétien reasoned, beyond a lot of telephone calls.

So Chrétien concluded he had a better claim to the leadership, and he ran, and collided with the big fix, and the Liberals broke his heart anyway, while slathering him with expressions of love and admiration.

In leadership conventions, as in elections, there are no second prizes, so when the 3,423 Liberal delegates handed Turner the prime ministership of Canada, he took it all—all the power, all the perquisites, all the prestige.

He would put it all at risk in an early election, but that was Trudeau's doing for staying so long and using up so much of the mandate won in 1980.

An early election could be advantageous, to cash in on

the convention publicity, carefully managed to make much out of little. By the end of the leadership campaign, the media had turned critical of Turner, as always happens after reporters feel they have been conned, but it didn't matter.

Turner had it—the prize that had been snatched away from John Diefenbaker, denied to Robert Stanfield, given and then withdrawn from Joe Clark. The office that politicians across the land crave in vain, was handed to Turner on a platter.

Turner announced he would give up his corporate directorships and work full-time at being prime minister. He would give up his law partnership, his table 23 at Winston's. He would move to Ottawa, all expenses paid. He would be as beautiful at 24 Sussex as Jeanne Sauvé was in the house across the street.

What's past, he said, was finished and done with. Let us look to the future.

A glance back, sir, without your permission. Is it not a fact that those who ignore the past are doomed to relive it?

2

MEMORIES OF BLUE EYES

I remember John Turner as the member for St. Lawrence-St. George in Montreal, and then Ottawa-Carleton, so we have a parliamentary track record to judge by, more detailed than we had on Pierre Trudeau when he came to power, or Joe Clark, or Brian Mulroney.

This was Turner, the very visible prime minister in waiting, and nothing in his political life was so vivid as the manner of his leaving it. When he went, in 1975, he protested his love of Parliament and his respect for the institution, and I asked him how he could say those things without giving us the reason for his going. He didn't just go—he went scorning his riding and his party, and he let the Ottawa-Carleton seat fall to the Conservatives and Jean Piggott without raising a hand to save it.

We said at the time that the old deathseat job of minister of finance had taken its toll again, and I recalled the day Turner was sworn into that job, a cold January 28 in 1972, when I met him in the washroom at Government House where he was taking off his overshoes, and asked whatever possessed him to take it.

He smacked his lips the way he does and said that when his leader asked him to do something, he did it.

Did it not seem a trap set for him by Trudeau?

He paused, smiled that non-smile of his where the eyes stay cold, and said it was just his duty. Just that.

When he was gone, I remembered only two things he had said as a cabinet minister. One was that we should be careful about change for the sake of change. The other was that 90 per cent of government classified documents could safely be made public—the difficulty was to identify the 10 per cent that shouldn't. Oh, yes, there was one thing more.

There was his insistence, in a series of budgets that set the stage for today's deficits, that the middle class deserved consideration, since they carried the bulk of the taxation load and generated the revenues that made Big Government possible.

Not bad stuff, in a country where most politicians leave little impression when they go, and make little impression when they are in office.

But pale stuff, surely, beside the utterances and actions of Pierre Trudeau—even keeping in mind that in one global book of quotations there are only two entries under T for Trudeau, and both of them are from Margaret.

Pierre Trudeau. To Turner, Old Pete. The convention that chose Turner paid tribute to Trudeau, extravagant tribute that brought water to the eye of many a Grit, and even some of us who had spent sixteen years as Trudeau watchers.

There stood Trudeau, looking better than he had when he took office in 1968. The man of a million photographs, none of them bad, none of them clumsy, none of them ungraceful.

The wisps of hair had hung on well, and the seams in his face were lines of character. The bags beneath his eyes bulged only occasionally, and never sagged. The midriff had barely thickened.

He had been to the bottom of the popularity pit, reviled, hated, and threatened with assassination to the point where he was guarded almost as tightly as the president of the United States, that office that had led so many of its occupants to their deaths.

Having tried everything there was to propose at home,

having preached (and saved) national unity until Canadians were as weary of it as they were of bilingualism, he determined on one last turn on the world stage.

When all else fails, said Machiavelli, distract their attention.

Trudeau had turned Canadian minds from the worst depression since the 1930s by patriating the Constitution and entrenching a sadly-compromised Charter of Rights, so diluted that Trudeau himself doubted its efficacy.

Now, he would seek to repair his own fortunes with a spontaneous peace initiative, whether his fellow world leaders were ready for it or not. He believed in it, and felt he had enough steam left to make it work, as the senior elected head of government in the world.

Successful politicians, as much as failed ones, live in a world of fantasy, surrounded by self delusions, some grand, some petty.

Trudeau started by dusting off the name of his illustrious predecessor, Lester Pearson (my own nominee for Canadian of the century), Canada's only winner of the Nobel Peace Prize, long envied by John Diefenbaker and Paul Martin, and now eyed by Trudeau.

Trudeau had turned away from Pearson and his works in 1968, giving the Liberals the new image that brought a majority government—something that Pearson had never been able to achieve.

Out went the "honest broker" role.

Out went NATO—almost.

Out went the good neighbour policy toward the United States, and in came a degree of *rapprochement* with the Soviet bloc unmatched in any other Western democracy.

Trudeau had tried everything—East-West dialogue, Pacific Rim diplomacy, up with China, up with Castro, up with Salvador Allende. Finally, it was back to Pearson, and peace.

Peace. To today's world it was what motherhood used to be, before the pill. The eternal dream, beyond criticism, beyond suspicion.

Trudeau had once called Pearson the unfrocked prince of peace for adopting nuclear warheads for the Bomarc missiles on Canadian soil, in line with our continental defence undertakings to the United States.

Now, that same Trudeau was agreeing to test the U.S. cruise missile in Canadian skies, and setting out to preach peace in the capitals of the world, as Pearson had before him.

Trudeau slipped through a new name for Toronto International Airport: Lester B. Pearson. He asked for Pearson references in his speeches.

And hither and thither in the world he flew, with everybody being polite, and nobody paying attention, except for the folk at home who read of his travels with mixed pride and puzzlement.

At the gates of 24 Sussex, he became the only world leader anywhere to be cheered by peace demonstrators. In Princeton, New Jersey, the judges were getting ready to award him the Albert Einstein Peace Prize, worth $50,000.

The peace initiative stirred the public opinion polls, those new versions of the Ten Commandments, lifting Trudeau from the depths and reversing a two-year drop that boosted the Tories to heights beyond those achieved by Diefenbaker at his peak. Trudeau's eyes brightened. Might he not stay on for another election, then quit while he was ahead, full of years and full of honours?

Chief Secretary Tom Axworthy put the machinery in motion for one more Trudeau-led election. He wrote a manifesto and video-taped it himself—Trudeau is our leader, we shall not be moved!

That tape was played to the youth wing of the party at the Turner convention, and everybody cheered. Axworthy edited out Trudeau's name, but left everything else in, hoping for a carry-over of Trudeau policies, and perhaps personnel, including himself.

But even as he taped it, before Trudeau's walk in the blizzard, it wasn't enough. Party pressures, caucus pressures, personal pride, a desire to seek his own pleasures while his body was still up to them, all led to Trudeau's decision to go.

There was one last reason to delay—Trudeau's hatred of John Turner, richly reciprocated.

Trudeau had ignored Lester Pearson after succeeding him, but he had at least acknowledged Pearson's existence, if not his accomplishments. He committed Turner to the land of the living dead after Turner quit the cabinet. He eliminated Turner from his mind as utterly as he had done earlier with the departing Robert Winters and Paul Hellyer.

Trudeau's record of mismanaging people is part of legend; his lack of compassion and human understanding is as prodigious as his fabled survivability, except perhaps where his own children are concerned, and we can't even be sure about that, if we are to believe Margaret's published accounts.

Neither Trudeau nor Turner has spoken frankly about what the 1975 split was about, though they have their own versions of what it was not about. Turner's version that Trudeau blocked a voluntary approach by labour to wage-and-price controls provoked a savage denial from Trudeau, and the two men agreed to disagree at the height of Turner's leadership drive.

My own feeling is that Mrs. Geills Turner hated being Number Two to Margaret Trudeau, a reaction shared by all cabinet wives, whose own places in the capital's social structure were wrecked by Mrs. Trudeau's upsetting of apple carts, and her cries of "goody, goody" along the way.

In Mrs. Turner's case, the situation was particularly galling because of her own, and her husband's, aspirations to be Number One.

Besides, the Turners were beautiful people, and Toronto was the place to blossom, to be admired and lionized, and also to be paid—the Turners needed to accumulate some serious money to keep them in the style to which they had been accustomed all their adult lives. Four hundred thousand a year might just do it.

Now, nine years later, could Trudeau head off the Turner succession?

He did, once, in 1979 when the prize was merely the

leadership of the opposition, and Turner spurned it. That time, the successor would have been Donald Macdonald, another Anglo who had taken an early quit from the Trudeau cabinet in favour of the Bay Street boardrooms. Macdonald had been one of the early Trudeaumaniacs in 1968, and had retained Trudeau's respect, if not affection, through his years in politics and after.

But for "Thumper," 1979 was too soon, and 1984 was too late, even though he had kept his leadership option open when Trudeau named him to head the most expensive, and most foolishly conceived, royal commission in the long history of such follies.

Who, then?

3

THE FIX

It was the turn of *les Anglais*, after sixteen years of Liberal leadership by a Quebecker.

But Trudeau had driven all the bright Anglos away, and there was no English-speaker of stature in his cabinet, nor had there been for years, or at least since Allan MacEachen self-destructed as minister of finance.

The strongest man in the cabinet was Marc Lalonde, but he was a Quebecker with as much political appeal as a pickle.

The most popular minister was Jean Chrétien, to judge by the eagerness of audiences from coast to coast to hear him speak. As Chrétien was to say, that was a hell of a lot of rubber chicken for the party—but by no stretch of the imagination could Chrétien sound as though English was his mother tongue.

Trudeau owed more to Chrétien than to any other minister, but he had never acknowledged the debt, either by publicly thanking the man, or buying him a drink, or even taking him to lunch.

Chrétien, for his part, never complained, never explained, never coveted a closer relationship with the man he called "the boss." Alone, among cabinet ministers, he honed his media relations and was a regular at the National

Press Club, where he cultivated the art of seeming to share confidences without ever disclosing anything.

Could Chrétien make it, and perhaps head off the dreaded Turner, who used to talk irreverently of Trudeau, calling him "Pete" behind his back, and worse things too, when media intimates would gather in his office?

Soundings were taken.

Yes, Chrétien would run—he had planned to do so all along, ever since the start of Trudeau's fourth mandate in 1980. But would the party accept him?

Probably not. Too French, too emotional, not enough class.

So, what to do?

For the Trudeauites, a way of living with Turner had to be found. Could Turner bring himself to speak well of Trudeau?

More soundings.

Yes, Turner could, and would—at the convention. And during the leadership campaign, he would go easy on the proud PET—or as easy as he could, considering his need to rebuild his own political persona and chart new directions.

Both Trudeau and Turner had in their minds the scene in 1979, when Trudeau, in defeat, announced his retirement and Turner considered running.

Turner confided to members of the Trudeau cabinet that he feared Trudeau would oppose his candidacy and campaign against him openly.

A mutual friend, who was in the cabinet, broached the matter with Trudeau on Turner's behalf, and word came back that if Turner ran, Trudeau would not openly oppose him. He would not endorse him publicly, but he wouldn't knock him, either.

In the end, Turner elected not to run, the prospect of opposition leadership not being attractive enough to divert him from the pursuit of pleasures and profit in Big T.O. and the boardrooms of the land.

That was one of Turner's most propitious decisions, because as soon as he had announced it Trudeau changed his mind about quitting, in the process destroying the leadership ambitions of at least two eager would-be candidates, Macdonald and Lloyd Axworthy.

As an extra added bonus Trudeau short-circuited colleagues who had applauded his decision to step down—Judd Buchanan, Robert Andras, Hugh Faulkner. The only doubter to survive that carnage inside the party was Jeanne Sauvé, who was sentenced, for her sins, to be speaker of the new House of Commons.

Never was anybody less suited, temperamentally, intellectually or by inclination to occupy the speaker's chair. Never did anybody flounder so at the start, then find her feet, and by sheer perseverance triumph in an unruly Parliament. And baby, look at her now!

Jeanne Sauvé once told me that she had never really fought an election in her life. She said the same thing about Pierre Trudeau and Marc Lalonde and all that horde of Quebec Liberal MPs whose election to the House of Commons was automatic once they were nominated as Liberals—Health Minister Monique Bégin's majority in the Montreal riding of St. Leonart Anjou in 1980 was typical: Bégin 42,205, NFP 3,741, PC 2,967.

You can't call that fighting an election, said Sauvé, and it brought to Ottawa a raft of Quebec MPs who not only kept the Liberal Party in office, but who had a warped idea of what politics was all about, particularly in terms of patronage.

Madame Sauvé agreed that the same could be said about Western Tory MPs whose election was guaranteed, especially in Alberta, but she said there was a difference, inasmuch as the Liberals seemed to be perpetually in power.

So it seemed, though nobody agreed on the reason why.

It was not that the party had any fixed philosophy, though its roots were in reform and it could point to a series of progressive policies put into force in the mid-twentieth century that marked it as a left-of-centre party. But similar policies were put into effect throughout the democratic world, and much that was done in Canada was copied from the anti-depression measures of Franklin D. Roosevelt in the United States. Copied not by a Liberal government, mind you, but by the Conservative government of that rabid old Tory, R.B. Bennett.

Pierre Trudeau, when he ran for the Liberal leadership, called himself a pragmatist, however much his critics might suspect him of socialist leanings carried over from his flirtation with the forces of the left.

He improvised as he went along, which is why the British press dubbed him "trendy." He bent with the winds that were blowing at the time, sometimes in tune with public opinion (the War Measures Act) and sometimes leading it (the Constitution). His personal philosophy was to go against the current and always seek to swim upstream, but you couldn't detect it in his actions as prime minister.

It had been the same with Lester Pearson, of whom it was said that he ran the government by the seat of his pants and was always happiest in times of crisis, which meant his years as prime minister were happy ones, indeed.

Whatever the Liberal coalition amounted to, nobody seemed sure, except that it was built on the rock of Quebec and all those automatic seats. The party came to be called the most successful instrument of democracy in the entire world, in terms of years in power. The Grits governed so long under Mackenzie King that whole generations of Canadians grew to maturity without ever knowing any other stripe of government. The switch to Louis St. Laurent prolonged the tenure by ten years, and after the Diefenbaker aberration, Pearson and Trudeau put together twenty-one more years of Liberal rule.

The Conservatives have to share some of the blame for this distortion of our parliamentary democracy into a one-party state.

It was not for nothing that we coined the phrase, years ago, that "Grit times are dull times, but Tory times are hilarious."

Partly, it was that the Conservatives were a truly national party in the sense of English Canada, so they had much to argue about among themselves, and they did.

And partly it was the leaders the Tories kept electing.

King versus John Bracken was no contest, any more than King versus Arthur Meighen had been earlier.

St. Laurent versus George Drew was a laugh—who in Canada would vote for Mr. Ontario?

Diefenbaker united the Conservative party briefly, and seemed to unite the whole country along with it—but the whole thing blew part, leaving scars on party and country that endure to this day, twenty years later.

Pearson versus Diefenbaker was a fair fight between two vastly different personalities—for those of us who write about such things, that was the golden age of political controversy and human drama in the House of Commons.

But then came the mismatch of Pierre Trudeau and Robert Stanfield, followed by Trudeau versus Joe Clark, and the brief surge of Tory hope when Clark won a minority mandate and made the enormous mistake of trying to govern as though he had a majority, and that was the end of him. "Lucky Pierre" got another crack, and another majority, and I despaired of ever again covering a federal government that wasn't Grit.

I even said a few prayers on the subject—Dear Lord, let me just once see a government that is not Liberal—and I don't count Diefenbaker or Clark because I'm not sure what they were. Just give someone else a try, just once, for the country's sake as well as my own.

I don't suppose God cares, and he certainly has never seemed disposed to answer my prayer and its part about the national welfare, based on my observation of what happens when a single party is in power for too long. The party had governed for so long, in fact, that its leaders and its members had come to think of clinging to power as the main reason for the party's existence, and as the means for perpetuating the Liberal fraternity.

What happens is that the whole apparatus of Big Government becomes adjusted to Liberal ways. The whole thing becomes a giant lump of patronage, justified by the conviction that Liberals know best and that all other parties contain nothing but idiots and blackguards.

Our political system was designed to work best when

there is the occasional change of party in power. This is the vital alternation—not, as the Liberals believe, the rotation of their leadership four times in the century between English and French.

There seemed a chance it might happen in 1984, when the Conservatives had themselves a leader who could stand toe to toe with Pierre Trudeau, or with John Turner, and who could boast that if he could keep his own fractious party united, he could do the same for the country. Nobody was sure just what Brian Mulroney's philosophy was, but then they had never been sure of Liberal leaders', either— certainly not Trudeau's, the philosopher king whose kingly tendencies were so much more pronounced than his philosophical ones.

Mulroney won his leadership in a convention that was exciting, just as the Trudeau convention in 1968 had been. But the Turner convention was contrived and scripted, so much so that it left a bad taste in a lot of Liberal mouths.

It seemed a hell of a way to choose a prime minister, but since the Liberals do it on an average of only five times in a century, it's tolerable.

What it is, like many things in Canadian politics, is a combination of ingredients taken from the British and American systems. The trouble is our propensity to pick the worst in each, and deny ourselves the best.

The system of political conventions is peculiarly part of politics in the United States, and they have had it for a very long time. We patterned our federal system on theirs and adapted it to our needs, diminishing the democratic process along the way, notably through the federal-provincial conference.

In the business of choosing political leaders, we veered away from the old British system where the choice was made by the parliamentary caucus, and we adopted the American hoopla convention. Trouble was, we had no way of giving the public at large a say, the way the Americans do with their complex system of primaries and caucuses. Their system is cumbersome and time consuming, and it drains the energies of the aspirants to leadership. Our way is shorter and more brutal, but in the end we wind up with leaders being chosen by some 3,500 partisans elected, or selected, by diverse means depending upon what part of the country they come from. The process is further distorted by the large number of automatic delegates and the imposition of quotas to court the votes of women and the young.

All the bad, old tricks that we have weeded out of our election procedures are there: money, manipulation, patronage, the buying and selling of support, the favour-seeking, the paying-off of old scores.

The Conservatives are better at it because they do it more often, and never when they are in power. With them, the prize doesn't carry the prime ministership with it, so they can be more relaxed, to the point of impeaching the youngest leader they have ever had, because he lacked chin, and replacing him with a man of no political experience, with a chin like a cowcatcher.

With the Tories, in every case except the choice of John Diefenbaker in 1956, the winner has wound up crowned with thorns, and even the Old Chief felt the prickles and the pricks after winning the biggest victory ever.

With the Liberals, the business of choosing a leader is called the race for the rose. Roses are red, you see, and by any other name would smell as sweet, and a rose is a rose is a rose. In this case, it was the rose Pierre Trudeau clutched between his teeth when he won in 1968, and the rose he wore in his lapel every day since then, and the rose Margaret refused to be in her husband's lapel. Let the Tories have their humble cornflower, let them colour themselves blue to match their usual mood.

The Liberals convened for their convention in a capital carpeted with rose petals, and there was a rose in every buttonhole, in every corsage. They painted the town bright red, and they wore red jackets and red pants and red hats and red underwear. And some would bleed, and that would be red, too.

4

WHELAN

SPREADING THE MANURE

We start with Eugene Whelan, the last man into the Liberal leadership contest, and the first out.

Whelan spoke the truth when he said he was the most easily recognized politician in Canada. And he was right when he said he knew his job better than any other minister—agriculture was his field, and he cultivated it thoroughly. Never once, in all his years, did the opposition trip him up on a question.

His answers were sprinkled with double negatives and usually ended with "egg-cetera, egg-cetera, egg-cetera," but he knew his stuff and farmers tended to respect him. Trouble was, there were no longer enough farmers to make a difference, at least not at a Liberal leadership convention.

John Crosbie had a marvellous description of Whelan—a combination of a leprechaun and a water buffalo.

Patrick Nagle of Southams described Whelan's speaking style as having "the broad public appeal of a backhoe calling its mate."

James Rusk of the august Toronto *Globe and Mail* wrote: "As with many a populist politician with little formal education, logic flows from anecdote rather than axiom, statistics flit into his speeches like unidentified flying objects and the language is stretched to new limits for a laugh."

Windsor, the city that earlier gave birth to Martinese—
the pompous linguistic convolutions of Paul Martin—now
spawned the bastard Whelanese, whose author thickened
it up the closer he got to any one of the nation's disappear-
ing barnyards.

Richard Cleroux of the *Globe* wrote that "trying to get
an answer from Eugene Whelan is like going to the St.
Lawrence River for a cup of water; you always get your
cupful and it does nothing to diminish the flow."

He was quoted as saying that, when he was a kid, he
was a poor student and a hell-raiser, and "the other kids
called me Nig or Coonie because I have dark skin and used
to have short, curly hair. Played softball with a couple of
black guys and they called me that, too."

And then there was Whelan's statement that people in
Africa have low IQs because they roast their brains by not
wearing hats in the sun. Whelan said he was really talking
about malnutrition in Africa and that he intended no racial
slur. Prime Minister Trudeau came to his defence and
recalled that Tory Crosbie had once chided Allan Mac-
Eachen for "going to Gabon with people who are swinging
from trees."

And the president of the National Dairy Council, Kemp-
ton Matte, said of Whelan: "The man can talk about any
subject, is amazingly well read and he gets well briefed. If
you're not prepared to meet him on a political issue, he'll
just blow you out the window."

In his green Stetson, he was a spectacle. He spewed
out speeches by the dozen. No other cabinet minister
spoke half as often, or used government jets half as much.

Whelan came through as the clown of the Trudeau
cabinet and the laughing stock of the convention, and the
kindest thing said about his candidacy was that he did it for
the fun.

Like hell he did. At heart, Whelan was one of those
Grandma Moses type radicals, similar to Bryce Mackasey
who, under the guise of moderate reform, once converted
the unemployment insurance plan into an agency for income redistribution, and dubbed himself a modern Robin
Hood.

Canadians have been paying for Mackasey's revolutionary act ever since, just as they will pay for Whelan's obsession with marketing boards and fixed prices for farm products.

Whelan, in fact, was not so much a clown as a small-c communist with a heart of gold, and the rest of us can be thankful that he was immobilized by the greatest social revolution ever to hit the country: urbanization. In Whelan's lifetime, the percentage of Canadians in rural areas dropped from 60 to less than 10—Whelan put the number of true farmers at about 6 per cent.

That switched the agriculture portfolio from one of the most important to one of the least, even though Whelan pleaded, rightly, that food was more vital than ever, and more endangered. He boasted, correctly, about the performance of what he called the agribusiness in Canada, and he called it the nation's most vital industry, and he said Canada was a world leader in food quality and farm productivity. All of this was true, but nobody listened. Nor did anybody pay attention when Whelan became head of the World Food Council, and was received twice in three months by the Pope. Whelan responded by dubbing himself the best-known politician not only in Canada, but in the world, and in one last fling he presided over a World Food Council meeting in Ethiopia, the very week Liberal delegates were gathering in Ottawa.

Nobody who heard Whelan's pleas on behalf of starving millions in the Third World could regard the man as a lightweight, or a full-time buffoon. He had held elected office for more than a quarter century, and had won eight times in the riding of Essex-Windsor.

Coincidentally, he was a Roman Catholic, a good omen for political success in today's Canada, as demonstrated by Pierre Trudeau, Jeanne Sauvé, Brian Mulroney, Joe Clark, Allan MacEachen, and even Whelan's fellow townsman and leadership candidate, Mark MacGuigan.

For two years, as an attention-getting device for my newspaper column, I had been touting the candidacy of Eugene Whelan for the Liberal leadership.

I did it partly to annoy the Liberals, my feeling being that if I was going to have to write about Grits in power for the rest of my life, I might as well have some sport. And it was partly because of my sincerely held feeling that Whelan knew his job. Too well, because there could be no doubt that if given power the man could be a menace. And I had no doubt from the moment he put on that green Stetson that he intended to run for the leadership.

Those Whelan columns were fun, and caused much mirth in press circles, where the very idea of a Whelan candidacy was a howl.

A few days after Trudeau announced his retirement, I had a call from Whelan's office. Had I been kidding about Whelan's candidacy, or was I serious? If he ran would I treat him seriously, or as a joke? Whelan was planning a press conference the next day and it seemed my answer would be important to his decision. My answer was that I was half laughing and half serious, and that if Whelan ran he would get his head knocked off and be humiliated. I was thanked and the Whelan press conference was postponed. There was one more phone call, and I made the same responses, days later.

Trudeau had made his announcement on Sadie Hawkins Day, February 29. On March 8, Donald Johnston announced his candidacy; on March 11, Mark MacGuigan; on March 13, John Roberts; on March 16, John Turner; on March 20, Jean Chrétien; on March 22, John Munro.

It was not until Thursday, April 12, that Whelan entered the contest, and I hailed him as the old manure spreader, the spittin' image of Benito Mussolini, the man who made Jean Chrétien's English sound good.

"I know the world as good as anyone," he proclaimed.

On technology, he said nobody knew more about genes than Gene, and genes are big in agribusiness.

He could out-weld all the other candidates, electric or acetylene.

As agriculture minister, he said "We've did it all, without increasing our budget."

But the Farm Credit Corporation had enjoyed "the

largest expansion it's ever saw in its history."

He was running "to win—I thought I outlined that pretty clear."

Previous agriculture ministers, like Joe Green, couldn't tell a sow from a cow.

He was unspoiled by his long years as a minister—"I don't act any different." The future was "a long ways away," and the leadership campaign "ain't no beauty contest; I don't pretend to be no Pierre Elliott Trudeau; you don't have no trouble identifying me...put my name in there and spell it right, and it ain't going to hurt me."

What about French? "I go to Quebec lots and never been received other than excellent. Once I give a speech in French."

He delayed his entry into the fray until he saw how many other candidates shot themselves in the foot, and now that "they jest may have grazed themselves," he was in.

And if there was a single theme in his campaign, it was that John Turner must not win. Turner the quitter, Turner the agent of Bay Street, Turner the pretty boy, must not win. He had beaten pretty boys before, in his own riding— "when the Tories saw their good-looking lawyer was beaten by a fat ugly son-of-a-bitch of a farmer they all came over to our side and they're still here."

5

MUNRO

THE BULLFROG CANDIDATE

The next-to-last man into the leadership contest was John Munro, and everybody wondered why.

Everybody except Munro, that is.

He had no trouble identifying himself as the friend of labour, the friend of the aboriginal peoples, the candidate of the left wing of the Liberal Party, and the foe of bankers, of Bay Street, of those who, as he put it, would repeal the twentieth century.

Munro saw himself as the man who could stop John Turner. As things turned out, he barely beat Eugene Whelan.

Everything was against Munro's candidacy from the start, and everything stayed that way to the finish, as his critics had predicted it would.

His misfortunes were recounted in song and story, and at the annual Press Gallery dinner, to the tune of "Harbour Lights," we sang:

> *I saw those harbour lights,*
> *In Hamilton the boys were dredging*
> *I phoned a judge that night,*
> *But he hung up on me.*
> *Then I knew lonely nights*

The PM said he had to fire me
And so one smokey night
I fired my office too.
I've fought a round or two
But, buddy, here's the rub
I stepped into the ring
But it was in the tub

(clenched teeth)

Now I take dainty bites
The docs of Hamilton re-wired me
Turn on those harbour lights
And let me shine for you!

That song set a course record for zingers—the harbourgate dredging scandal in Hamilton, Munro's resignation for phoning a judge on behalf of a constituent, a fire in Munro's parliamentary office traced to a chain-smoked butt, Munro's unexplained fall in the bathtub that saw him return to Ottawa bruised and battered, with his jaw wired shut, mouthing that the press had no mercy.

Indeed, the press had none, and Munro took sweet revenge when the *Toronto Sun* fabricated a story about his alleged involvement in the government's takeover of Petrofina, and he collected $75,000 in damages.

Since then, the media has handled Munro with tongs, which is one reason his leadership candidacy got so little coverage. Munro kept crying foul, but in fact there was little positive to say, and the negative didn't seem worth recounting.

In vain did Munro liken his candidacy to that of Gary Hart in the United States. (Munro and Mark MacGuigan ended in a tie for Gary Hart references to themselves.)

In vain did he espouse the cause of the native peoples and count on them for his delegate base at the convention. And though he articulated the tenets of the left more forcefully than any other candidate, the rightist lean of the times made him sound futile, and almost quaint.

Munro's physical stance, sitting or standing, was unappealing. With his head tucked deep into his shoulders, hunched forward, face distorted into a scowl, it might have been possible to liken him to a Churchillian bulldog. Instead, the image invoked was that of a bullfrog.

The puzzling thing about John Munro was that, while he failed to impact on Ottawa or across the land, he was strong in his native Hamilton, and consistently won in a working class riding that should have been a bastion of the New Democratic Party.

Media, including home-town media, kept criticizing, and there were constant innuendos about the company Munro was keeping in high circles and low. Always, he survived, and the impression grew through the years that he was unbeatable.

It was a notion that deceived Munro himself into thinking he could run for the leadership without risking humiliation, as the voice of the true liberalism that had kept the party in office for so much of the century, excepting only the decade of the First World War, the five worst years of the Great Depression, the Diefenbaker phenomenon, and the Joe Clark burp.

Munro attacked the banks. He pledged to strengthen the Foreign Investment Review Agency. He went after fellow candidates Turner and Donald Johnston for neo-conservatism, and said voters would prefer the real thing, Brian Mulroney. He said there should be no compensation to Canadian Japanese for wartime wrongs, and sought the money for wrongs committed against the native peoples.

He defended the right of the poor to play the lotteries, and he took campaign contributions from Manitoba Indians who were receiving heavy federal subsidies.

Through it all, Munro gave the impression of being a blubberer, a crybaby. Indeed, reporters had seen him cry with anguish when he offered his resignation to Trudeau in 1975 when his name was raised in the Hamilton dredging case, and he wept again when he resigned in 1978 for having telephoned the judge.

In the end, John Munro's leadership candidacy served no useful purpose, to himself or to the party, and his reasons for running remained as obscure as those of that other dark horse candidate, Mark MacGuigan.

6

MACGUIGAN

DEATH BY DEGREES

Mark-a-mark-a-mark-a-mark-a-mark-a-mark-a-ma-Guigan,
Send me some dough, I'm running low, oh, oh!
Boy George parody, April, 1984.

Mark MacGuigan put himself forward as the thinking man's candidate for the Liberal leadership.

Trouble was that when he himself was lost in thought, he had an unfortunate tendency to close his eyes, whereupon the photographers took his picture.

Even wide awake, his gaze was walleyed. And when he spoke, audiences either stayed away, or dozed.

A devout Roman Catholic, he was separated from his wife and, as minister of justice, he was seeking to liberalize the divorce laws.

Pierre Trudeau had caught on, years before, by saying the state had no place in the bedrooms of the nation. MacGuigan changed bedrooms to boardrooms, and it didn't click.

What would make such a man think he was qualified to become Liberal leader and prime minister?

Many things, said MacGuigan.

Louis St. Laurent had been external affairs minister and justice minister before becoming prime minister.

Lester Pearson had been minister for external affairs.

And Pierre Trudeau had been justice minister.

MacGuigan had headed both external and justice, so why shouldn't he run?

He had inherited his Windsor riding from Paul Martin, who had run twice for leadership. Martin supported MacGuigan, so why not go for it?

He had politics in his blood; his father had been a Liberal cabinet minister in Prince Edward Island for ten years, followed by a twenty-three-year tenure as a Supreme Court judge in the island province.

He himself was a distinguished academic, with a string of six degrees. And he had the common touch, an intellectual elected five times in an industrial riding, his 1980 majority of over 6,000 being his largest ever.

His proposed criminal code reforms had been praised in the legal community. His moderate views on United States foreign policy had tempered Trudeau's testiness. His early espousal of multiculturalism had endeared him to ethnics, and won him the support of Edmonton Mayor Laurence Decore, who offered his city as a launching pad for MacGuigan's candidacy.

Decore said of MacGuigan that "most politicians blow with the wind—he sets the direction the wind blows."

A nice image, but MacGuigan couldn't sustain it.

Once, he opposed official bilingualism for Ontario. Now, he supported it.

He campaigned on a platform of full employment without ever making clear how he would go about it, saying only that it would be done by the private sector, not the government.

He said he had potential support inside the parliamentary caucus and among New Brunswick delegates, "but they haven't ripened enough so that I can announce them yet." In fact, they never did.

He turned on media in his exasperation, chiding reporters for writing stories downgrading his chances. On

April 17, in Montreal, he said: "You've written for a month that I've nothing in Quebec. You should be surprised that I'm neck-and-neck with Turner, if not ahead."

If not, indeed.

He accused the press of giving too much coverage to John Turner and Jean Chrétien, saying: "My only problems are with the press. We're not getting equal time. The media owes it to all of us to treat us equally."

Two weeks later, on May 16, he was saying that some candidates should consider dropping out of the contest because of lack of support. He made it clear he wasn't talking about himself, because he knew he was running a strong third.

He said there was a clear chasm between his own economic policies and those of John Turner, adding that this would be no bar to his swinging his support to Turner at the convention, since he was a free man.

MacGuigan was accused of running his leadership campaign out of his parliamentary office, at public expense. He canvassed other candidates for an agreement to hold campaign expenses down, but was ignored. Members of his campaign staff were accused of doubling as government employees.

On Global TV, interviewer Doug Small tricked MacGuigan into thinking the cameras were off during a commercial break, and then led the candidate into a light-hearted admission that he would fire Bank of Canada Governor Gerald Bouey. "Yellow journalism," protested MacGuigan.

Mayor Decore, an able campaigner himself, was driven to distraction by MacGuigan's inability to win support, and finally explained it was because MacGuigan was very shy, and that he was better one-on-one than with a crowd. Some of MacGuigan's rallies almost boiled down to that—his smallest crowd numbered five.

"Delegates," said MacGuigan, "see me as the candidate with the most growth potential."

Certainly, he had nowhere to go but up at the convention. But most of the delegates couldn't see him at all.

7

ROBERTS
BABYFACE AT FIFTY

The late, great Professor Frank Underhill once said that Canadian men are born old, and that they come into the world two drinks below par.

It follows that most Canadian men of thirty-five look and act fifty, while most men of fifty do well to look only ten years older than that. Our national yield of boy-men is phenomenally low, much lower than in the United States where the cast of youth can stay with a man into his seventies, sustained by a competitive thrust in sports and business that makes Americans the most envied, admired, and hated people in the world.

Our leading example of boy-manship has been Pierre Elliott Trudeau, whose physical and mental gifts bid fair to sustain him into his eighties and beyond. Not for nothing did fair Margaret say, ten years ago, that he had the body of a twenty-five-year-old, and he looks better today than he did then.

There were two other boy-men in the Trudeau entourage, and one of them need not concern us here. Not that Jim Coutts has no significance in our politics, and in the unfolding story of the party of perpetual power, the Liberals.

But on April 6, Coutts announced he would not be

running for the job of Liberal leader and prime minister, thereby saving himself from the fate of having his cute little head knocked off at the convention.

That leaves John Roberts, the fifty-year-old who looks thirty-five, the man who has always been around longer than anybody would think, to look at him.

The important part of the Roberts story opens in September of 1976, when Trudeau brought two bright boys from Toronto into his cabinet, to freshen things up for the future.

Into the ministry of consumer and corporate affairs went Tony Abbott, forty-five. And John Roberts, forty-two, became secretary of state.

Abbott had the lineage. His father, Doug, almost certainly could have succeeded Louis St. Laurent as Liberal leader, but chose instead to take a Supreme Court appointment in 1954, leaving the succession to Lester Pearson.

Roberts had the pizzazz, having risen from a humble upbringing to be a star scholar, diplomat, and politician, driven by an ambition to be prime minister.

Abbott fizzled, and is remembered chiefly for a memo he wrote to himself urging that he do better.

Roberts tried and tried, and eventually became the senior minister from Toronto, by dint of elbowing and kneeing other ministerial aspirants out of the way— especially James Fleming, who had the bad judgment to challenge the press barons of the land to a joust, and got unhorsed.

Now, Roberts himself faced a challenger out of the shadows, John Turner, and he had no option but to do battle and put forward his own claims to leadership. If he did not, and Turner won, he would be nowhere. If he did, and lost, he would be nowhere, too, but he would have given it a go.

Off he went, waging what many observers thought was the most eloquent of all the leadership campaigns, impressing delegates every time he spoke, even though they would not give him their votes. He looked people in the eye, and they said he levelled with them, and he spoke about the "new Liberalism" until it became a cliché, and media people winced every time the word "new" passed Roberts' lips. For Roberts, it was the only way to go, and he went, tagging Turner in the process as "yesterday's man."

Vainly did Roberts plead, when Turner's victory seemed more and more inevitable, that what he meant was that Turner would be marked as yesterday's man unless he could prove otherwise.

And vainly did Roberts try to appeal to the core of the Liberal party in the name of progress, posing as the candidate of youth. It helps if you look thirty-five, but the statistics said fifty.

The man had been around a long time, and the files on him contain this entry on Roberts' first election win, in 1968:

> By this time, Roberts had married his second wife, Beverley Rockett, a stunning former model and a professional photographer. His first wife, Brigitte, was an aristocratic Belgian who brought a trunkload of Dior dresses to Ottawa. She soon developed a dislike for things Canadian, including Roberts. The marriage was annulled and she returned to Europe. Roberts is 'amicably separated' from Rockett and still acts as stepfather to three children in their 20s from Rockett's previous marriage. All three worked in Roberts' leadership campaign.

All good, fashionable stuff in the Ottawa of 1984, where it is widely accepted that politics is the hardest profession of all on marriages, with the possible exception of medicine, and the news business.

The only problem Roberts had with his lifestyle, oddly enough, was countering the impression that he had been born with the same silver spoon in his mouth that John Turner had, and persuading people that he really knew what poverty and hard work were all about. Critics said he was lazy on the job—that was why he hadn't fulfilled Trudeau's hopes for him as an Anglo wunderkind.

Trudeau could argue that he did his best for Roberts, giving him two good cabinet vehicles—environment from

1980 to 1983, and then employment and immigation, a high-profile launching pad for a leadership bid. With these, together with his previous regime as cultural czar, Roberts should be able to fly.

He tried.

God knows, he tried. But with Toronto shot out from under him by Turner, there was no place to go, no growth to be had.

Roberts is just as "with it" as Turner, maybe more. He has his own table at Ottawa's smartest restaurant, to match Turner's at Winston's. He uses the lingo of the hour with more accuracy and currency than Turner does, and he is more reflective, not given to beating people on the back. And he laughs, at the world and at himself. He is a workaholic, but not a compulsive worker—sort of a cross, in this respect, between Pierre Trudeau's laid-back approach and John Turner's semi-panic.

Above all, in Roberts' campaign, there was a quiet elegance of phrase and eloquence of manner that marked him in the confrontation meetings and caused him to be classed as best, sustaining his illusion that he might win at the convention, or at least save something for the future.

No chance.

Because of the "newness" implied in the Turner candidacy (even though it seemed to be a kind of new conservatism), Roberts' "new Liberalism" theme didn't take off, though it deserved to, being in the tradition of King, St. Laurent, Pearson, and Trudeau.

The delegates fell for it when those leaders first called themselves "new," so why wouldn't it work now?

The reason is that it was so obviously a gimmick, so clearly lifted from candidate Gary Hart's presidential campaign in the United States. And Hart had copied it from John F. Kennedy, who had taken it from Franklin Roosevelt, who had pinched it from the ancient Greeks.

It was as though Roberts had prepared his speeches and then dropped the word "new" into every paragraph, to create the illusion of himself as tomorrow's man and the candidate of youth.

Even the young people, it turned out, wouldn't fall for it, so Roberts was left with the substance of his candidacy, which was considerable, leaving wistful thoughts about what might have been had Roberts made full use of his talents and opportunities.

Not in this century had a candidate for leadership summed up the meaning of his party so movingly—certainly, no one had done it in the Liberal campaigns of 1919, 1948, 1958, or 1968, nor had any Conservative ever described that party so truly, not even John Diefenbaker in 1956, when he changed it to fit his own strong image. Roberts' campaign was in the image of the Adlai Stevenson of 1952 and 1956, when he stirred the imaginations of Democrats but lost the country to Dwight Eisenhower.

For Roberts, there were too many Eisenhowers: Donald Johnston with his clumsy, drably expressed ideas of substance; Jean Chrétien with his tug at the heartstrings; John Turner with his promise of salvation from defeat.

Roberts stood accused of using a job-creation program as a slush fund, and of trying to short-circuit Tory MPs, in their own ridings with federal handouts. But he kept reaching for high ground in his campaigning, talking about the need for a new balance, based on social justice and a new set of economic strategies.

The party must not drift to the right—no new leader can be allowed to turn away from the old Liberal goals of individual opportunity, reform, and community.

These are the ''people'' issues, and Roberts was equally effective with women delegates, coming closest of all the men to seeing issues through their eyes.

Eyeing Chrétien, he said that dreams, continuity, and love of country are not enough to make a leader.

Addressing Turner, he warned that ''the leader is not the chief executive officer; Canada is not a limited company; we don't hire and fire citizens; the bottom line is not balance sheets, it's people.''

The Liberals buzzed about Roberts' speeches, and the manner in which he made them. Papers headlined that he was winning respect, but what he needed was votes.

Yes, he had lost two elections, but he didn't call them defeats. He said he had been "insufficiently appreciated."

Why was he running?

"Because there is just a chance, a smidgen of a chance, a mere possibility, an offside doubt, that Sinclair Stevens and John Crosbie and Brian Mulroney might take over the government of this country. If that doesn't rouse you up to a fighting spirit as a Liberal, nothing will."

Roberts, with degrees from the best universities in Canada, Britain, and France, totally bilingual, was battling against Johnston to be the Anglophone alternative to John Turner.

He perceived both Johnston and Turner as Liberals tiptoeing to the right, "come to their views by a process of discovery or education during the campaign."

He attacked the Canadian banks for failing to serve Canadians properly, especially Canadian women. Roberts so upset the Canadian Bankers' Association that they complained to Prime Minister Trudeau about "bank bashing" by his would-be successors, especially Roberts, Whelan, and Chrétien.

Roberts put out a policy paper on foreign affairs, defence, and disarmament that was the clearest statement to come from any Canadian politician since Pearson. He lauded Trudeau's ten principles for peace and concluded: "Mr. Trudeau's expertise and prestige in this area are so great that it would be a tragedy were he not to continue the efforts so successfully initiated. I would ask him to become a special Canadian ambassador for peace and disarmament to pursue these fundamental objectives."

Roberts complained when Turner's organization gave out 2,000 samples of imported perfume at a policy conference on Mother's Day.

He risked the wrath, and got it, of the public servants when he said many of them don't work hard enough and the federal bureaucracy should be reduced, combining the departments of labour and manpower, and folding the ministries of social and economic development into the Privy Council office.

He denied that he had used $1 million of taxpayers'

money for brochures aimed at youth and women, containing his photograph. He said it wasn't a very good picture, anyway.

He challenged other leadership candidates to debate on TV, but it didn't happen.

And he was criticized for what were called his well-dressed, upper-class style and looks, though he said he only goes to two cocktail parties a year. A colleague said that "even when he looks dishevelled, he never looks like it's from cutting down trees."

He worked the federal pork barrel in Metro Toronto, warning all the while that technological change could devastate Canadian society unless the federal government prepared for it quickly by drafting new programs.

In the past, he said, Canada enjoyed easy, automatic economic growth, based on manufacturing and resources. No more. There must be a shift from consumption to investment in both the private and public sectors, and tax changes to encourage Canadians to accumulate capital and invest it in Canadian enterprises.

Delegates agreed he was good to hear, and that they liked his ideas. But not enough, as it turned out. Not nearly enough. Roberts, who had given the business to cabinet colleague Jim Fleming, was about to get it himself, and there was no escape.

In the leadership contest, there were two candidates running for first place and five running for third—and at one state of the campaign it almost sounded as though third place was the top prize.

This approach originated in the Conservative convention of 1976, when Joe Clark came from third to defeat Claude Wagner and Brian Mulroney. As a convention strategy, running for third turned out to be a total delusion, but it gave the back of the pack a bit of credibility, at a time when reporters were writing about them as "the bozos."

The man who was to capture third place, for what it was worth, was Donald Johnston. He did succeed in winning the attention of a lot of people who had never noticed him—not for the way he said things, but for what he said.

The way he said things was unremarkable, except

when he wept at the thought of his daughters pleading to be spared nuclear war. What really brought his campaign alive was a tennis ball in the eye that gave him a shiner, whereupon his supporters blacked their own eyes and chanted that they would rather fight than switch. Johnston said he got the eye from a guy who mistook him for Brian Mulroney, and everybody perked up and asked who this tall guy was.

An odd-looking bird, with a head too small for his body, and a taste for show business, reflected in his ability to play piano, he could sing without any distinction, and he once wrote a perfectly dreadful song in praise of the government's six-and-five wage-and-price control program. Before winning the Westmount riding in a 1978 by-election when Bud Drury retired, he had been Pierre Trudeau's tax consultant, and had written a book proving that the tax laws were a crock. Trudeau loved it.

8

JOHNSTON
THE THIRD MAN

There was a lot to love in Donald Johnston, that elongated chimpanzee of a man with so much fire in his mind and so little in his belly.

How could a person that interesting be that dull?

The headlines mounted during his leadership campaign, and people came out to hear him, and went away shaking their heads. The man knew nothing about projection.

The strange thing is that he did know about merchandising, and about show business. He knew more about those things than he did about practical politics—practical in the sense that political ideas have to be brought off the paper if they are to become reality. If their author can't do that, then somebody else has to, as was done by the disciples of Jesus and Karl Marx.

The leadership campaign of Donald Johnston contained more policy proposals than most political leaders come up with in a lifetime.

He said the leadership must be contested on policy issues, and he held to that view to the finish, and he was wrong. The issue was settled on style, not substance—and while Don Johnston and his bulging briefcase of bright ideas would be at the disposal of the Turner government, he would not get the full rein he needed to put those ideas into action.

Johnston was the first man to declare his candidacy, eight days after Trudeau announced his intention to resign. He promised to stress issues and the search for new solutions to the technological revolution, and he said that, like everybody else, he was spooked by the Turner media juggernaut.

It took a while for people to notice Johnston, yet his life story is one of the most fascinating in Canadian politics.

Youngest leadership candidate, at age forty-six. Brought up in a farmhouse in Cumberland, outside Ottawa, where his self-educated mother taught him to read and write. Father comes home from the war, family moves to Ottawa and then to Montreal where, in a downtown rooming house, Johnston learns to play the piano.

Parents divorce (no connection, apparently, with son's piano lessons). He pays his way through high school taking care of tennis courts, and learns the game, using tennis tournaments as a route to university.

At McGill, shares an apartment with poet Leonard Cohen; is a classmate of Michael Pitfield.

Is admitted to law school by Dean Gerald Le Dain, now the newest justice of the Supreme Court of Canada. Wins gold medal as top student.

Wins fellowship to travel through Africa with other students in 1957. Fellow traveller is Pierre Elliott Trudeau, and they buddy up for the trip.

Back in Montreal, gets job offer from firm of Stikeman, Elliott. Making the offer is John Turner.

Joins firm, specializes in tax counselling, sets up own firm in 1966, a later partner being one Peter Blaikie, future national party president of the Conservative Party.

Devises motion picture tax shelters for investors. Romances Wendy MacLaren but, when Wendy takes a trip, switches to her twin sister Heather and marries her. Wendy marries Johnston's best friend, Graham Watt. Johnston has Trudeau as a tax client. Johnston writes a book called *How to Survive Canada's Tax Chaos*.

Quebec elects a Parti Québécois government, and Johnston decides to enter politics. Trudeau approves, and

Johnston wins the Westmount by-election in 1978, a year in which Tories were sweeping by-elections all over the country, except Quebec.

Johnston survived the Trudeau defeat of 1979, and when Trudeau regained power in the 1980 election, he made Johnston president of the Treasury Board. But in 1982, Trudeau denied Johnston his coveted crack at finance, giving the job instead to Marc Lalonde, and tucking Johnston away in the economic development portfolio, a job that Johnston quickly concluded was ripe for abolition.

Once he decided to contest the leadership, the policies started to pour out, and they didn't stop until the candidacy died on the convention floor—his delegates shouting to the end the most curious slogan of all: ''we're number three!''

Johnston proposed a guaranteed annual income for all Canadians aged nineteen to sixty-five, to replace unemployment insurance and other welfare programs, with pension schemes being preserved as is.

He favoured abortion on demand, saying it was a matter between a woman and her doctor.

He said new technology is a tidal wave, and that we must either ride with it or drown.

He called for revision of the national energy program, with Petro Canada selling off its gas stations, and a review of offshore oil subsidies.

He suggested giving chairmen of House of Commons committees some of the powers of cabinet ministers, and proposed more free votes in Parliament so regional MPs could better represent their areas.

He would reform the tax system so it would become a spur to the economy, not a drag.

He objected to the payment of bonuses to executives of the money-losing Crown corporations, de Havilland and Canadair.

Through all this, opposition critics kept calling for Johnston's resignation from the cabinet, and the calls reached a crescendo when Johnston, in Toronto, said the Trudeau government should scrap its main industrial grants program, all $2.5-billion worth of it. Yes, he had helped create the program, but he now felt it was just not working, that it was building on economic weaknesses rather than strengths, and propping up industrial losers.

"Did I hear you correctly?" asked one businessman.

"Yes, you did," said Johnston, registering a political first on the Richter scale.

Johnston was unrepentant, and Trudeau stood by the right of his minister to state his views, even when they conflicted with present government policy.

Johnston was on firmer ground with Trudeau when he proposed that Canada move aggressively to embrace the Soviets as a means toward nuclear disarmament.

He said his rival candidates were dishonest and gutless when they failed to face issues and accused him of taking the Liberal party to the right. An aide said Johnston's prime target, though unnamed, was John Roberts.

He called for substantial cuts in the federal public service, through the elimination of whole departments.

He said Canada's economic development could not be built around bureaucratic blueprints, and that entrepreneurship was the key.

He called for an end to federal-provincial squabbling, because Canadians were fed up with it. And he shrugged off suggestions that many of his own proposals challenged the traditional divisions of power between Ottawa and the provinces.

He rejected suggestions for a shorter work week without reduced pay, asking: "How on earth can you be more productive doing that?" But he proposed giving all Canadian workers the right to earn time off to take leave for education and training.

Great stuff, everybody agreed. Damn good man. Every party should have one. But as the convention date neared, what party notables had endorsed Johnston?

Failed renegades like Jim Fleming and Gildas Molgat, and MPs Jack Burghardt, David Berger, Paul McRae and Claude-André Lachance. Clearly, Johnston was a prophet without honour in the circle of caucus and cabinet, and he had more reason to grieve at this neglect than even the much-put-upon Jean Chrétien, the most abandoned man in Christendom, or at least in Quebec.

A word in passing about Jim Fleming, the one-time trusted pal of Pierre Trudeau who got caught between the rock of John Roberts' ambitions and the hard place of the publishers of the nation's newspapers, bent on his destruction.

Fleming was a communications expert who was first elected to Parliament in 1972, for the riding of York West, his win helping to give Trudeau his narrow victory margin. He took over the multicultural ministry in 1980, and Trudeau assigned him to the perceived crisis in the newspaper industry, manifest by concentration of ownership and closure of dailies. Fleming became a member of the top cabinet committee, priorities and planning, and set to work.

But Roberts, getting ready for his leadership move, shouldered Fleming off the cabinet committee, and became the top patronage dispenser in Metro Toronto.

By this time, the newspaper proprietors had Fleming's number, and were moving in for the kill.

Fleming's proposed Newspaper Act was designed to distil the findings of a royal commission on newspaper monopoly, and a subsequent court case that demonstrated the wide gaps in existing combines legislation. He talked, at the same time, of trying to ensure the independence of the nation's newsrooms from the influence of the owners, and he proposed government subsidies for a watchdog national press council, and the expansion of news coverage through bureaus at home and abroad.

Fleming's proposals summoned the nation's publishers to the ramparts, their voices raised to hitherto unprecedented heights, or depths, of indignation. Nor did the denizens of the newsrooms rally to Fleming's defence, or in support of any of his measures. Freedom of the press was at stake, and Fleming must be burned.

When it was over, Fleming was out of the cabinet, and his Newspaper Act was abandoned by the government that had spawned it.

On an April day, in the midst of the Liberal leadership campaign, a lonely figure rose in the House of Commons to submit a private member's bill, endorsed by nobody but himself.

It was Fleming, in his role as a backbencher, asking the Commons "to ensure, at the national level, competition and independence of the daily press."

The chamber was almost empty, and so were the public galleries, and the press gallery.

When Fleming had finished presenting his case against concentrated monopoly ownership, two government parliamentary secretaries proceeded to talk his bill to death.

Michel Veillette, parliamentary secretary to Consumer and Corporate Affairs Minister Judy Erola, said the new Combines Investigation Act would deal much more efficiently with the newspaper industry than Fleming's proposed Newspaper Act.

And Jack Burghardt, parliamentary secretary to Communications Minister Francis Fox, said the Trudeau cabinet never did have a hard and fast policy position on newspaper ownership, and that Fleming's original bill was no more than a document to stimulate discussion. He added:

"The government has taken the comments, views and wishes of those who have made representations regarding the original Daily Newspaper Act into consideration. That is perhaps the reason the legislation is not being presented by the government.

"Much was said on the part of daily newspaper publishers and editorial writers regarding this particular bill. I would suggest to the House that while much of this comment at the time perhaps seemed rather harsh and extremely critical of that particular act, many of those comments have been taken into account. That is one of the reasons this legislation was never introduced in Parliament."

Burghardt ended with a plea for special status for the owners of the *London Free Press*, who also own a television station, an AM radio station, and an FM station in that city.

He neglected to mention that he himself was a former on-air employee of the company.

Up rose another Liberal, David Berger, to say Fleming was wrong to suggest that concentration of ownership restricts freedom of the press and diversity of opinion.

"It may be," said Berger, "that concentration of ownership, in certain circumstances, may encourage a diversity of opinion. There is competition within a newspaper. We are all aware of the journalists who often take opposing views on the same subjects and we find their views on the same day, on the same page, of many newspapers."

And that was the end of Fleming and his bill, and nobody waved goodbye, because there was nobody there.

A footnote came in the form of a telephone call from somebody once close to Fleming: What did I think of Fleming's chances if he ran for the leadership?

I said he would get slaughtered, by delegates and newspapers alike.

And I drew the caller's attention to the fact that supposedly fearless commentators like myself had not addressed the question of newspaper closures and monopolies with the same relentless objectivity we bring to bear on prime ministers or questions of world peace, acid rain or federal-provincial relations. Leaning on my seniority, I had perhaps been more outspoken than most in the trade, but it was pallid stuff, perceived in stony silence by publishers, proprietors, and the public, of whom it has truly been said that they get the newspapers they deserve. My caller thanked me, and hung up.

The next thing I knew, Fleming had endorsed the candidacy of Don Johnston. And I listened to hear if Johnston would have anything to say about concentration of newspaper ownership.

He did not—perhaps because, among his backers, there were Jack Burghardt and David Berger, the very men who had hammered those last nails into Fleming's coffin.

And at the convention, they all went down together.

9

THE BIG GUY FROM SHAWINIGAN

If I were an Anglais,
Marc Lalonde could kiss my ass just like he did Pierre
*   Trudeau,*
Ministers won't treat me like a clown
If I were an Anglo-phown!

Parody, April, 1984

A further line had Jean Chrétien singing: "Alternance, it's driving me crazy."

And in the end, it did.

For Chrétien, once he was in and told his supporters to fasten their seatbelts for a hell of a ride, there was no escape. He was airborne, with no safe place to land, and so he crashed.

But oh, it was a wonderful hell of a ride, and it proved that a lot of Liberals had hearts, even though most of them didn't. He appealed to emotions most Liberals, and most Canadians, didn't know they had. A Quebecker who cared about Canada, the way John Diefenbaker had cared, with a catch in his voice and a maple leaf on his arm.

"These mountains are mine," Chrétien had proclaimed the first time he saw the Rockies. And he said the same about the peaks of Baffin Island, the fjords of Newfoundland, the beaches of Vancouver Island. He greeted the native peoples as brothers.

Chrétien, like Tory Leader Brian Mulroney, came from a blue-collar Quebec mill background. It was interesting that four of the seven Liberal aspirants boasted humble beginnings—Chrétien, Johnston, Whelan, and Roberts, outnumbering the children of privilege in the contest, Turner, MacGuigan, and Munro. That, for what it was worth, was a change from the Trudeau convention of 1968, or the Pearson convention of 1958, or the St. Laurent one of 1948, or that of Mackenzie King in 1919.

For Chrétien, the Little Guy from Shawinigan, it was worth everything through the campaign, though in the end it did him in. Humble beginnings and his common touch cost him the support of the Liberal Quebec elite, and with it whatever real chance he had to become leader, and prime minister.

First in our hearts, said party president Iona Campagnolo, though second in our votes. For the Liberals, there had not been so much talk about ''heart'' since the Tin Woodman of Oz.

Chrétien deserved it, for a bigger-hearted man had never come to Ottawa, certainly not from the backwater boonies of Quebec, dominated as they were when Chrétien was growing up by the owner-managers, *les Anglais*.

It was *les Anglais* who lived in the big houses, and the Chrétiens who lived in tarpaper shacks. It was *les Anglais* who owned the mills in which Papa Chrétien worked and sometimes held down as many as four jobs at the same time. It was *les Anglais* who never spoke French—why should Chrétien speak English?

If ever a man was deeply rooted on the French side of Quebec's two solitudes, it was Jean Chrétien—and yet he made a forcible entry onto the English side, learned the lingo, listened, and compelled people to listen to him.

When people ask me why I find Chrétien so attractive, I say he'd be a marvellous companion on a desert island, and

I've never said that about any other politician except John Diefenbaker.

Can you imagine being on a desert island with Pierre Trudeau?

Or John Turner?

They would be totally preoccupied with building a canoe as a means of escape. Chrétien would make the best of things, and keep his companions stimulated and laughing.

I would not have noticed Chrétien when he came to Parliament in 1963, except that he had wrested the St. Maurice riding away from the Créditistes, his margin being less than 2,000 votes. The Créditistes under Réal Caouette were riding high at the time, denying Liberals the seats that would have given Lester Pearson his majority.

At the time, I was the host of a CBC TV program called "The Sixties," and we wanted to do a program profiling bright new faces in the House of Commons, and two of the people chosen were Jean Chrétien and John Turner.

The kinescope of that program is now a historic document, and what I remember best about it was the way Chrétien could make himself understood with his halting English, and the enthusiasm he had for travelling around the country making appearances for any English-speaking Liberal MP who would have him.

Travel in those days was still largely by train, and we had shots of Chrétien sleeping in the waiting rooms of country railway stations, and hitch-hiking his way on country roads, and eating those first of the thousands of rubber chicken meals he boasted about in his leadership campaign. Chrétien kept up this pace for twenty-one years, partly because he enjoyed it, partly because he loved the country and the Liberal Party, and partly because he felt he was accumulating a pile of IOU's that would come in handy when he bid for the leadership.

In politics, all these attitudes are admirable, and so I admired Jean Chrétien.

When he was minister of Indian and northern affairs, I admired his futile effort to bring Canada's Indians into the mainstream of Canadian life, an offer they refused.

And in particular I admired his establishment of so many new national parks, including two in his native Quebec. There were objections to the park he was proposing on Vancouver Island, and I attended a meeting in Victoria in which he listened to the protesters, and then told them what the park would mean to future generations.

Remember, this was early in the assertion of the French Fact, yet here was a Quebecker telling British Columbians what would be good for them, and doing it on their own ground. It was one of the few times I have seen people change their minds because they believed what they were hearing, and believed the person who was telling them.

To this day, I cannot imagine an English-speaker going into Quebec and, in flawed French, persuading a doubting crowd about anything. I once tried to explain to Marc Lalonde why it was that he put Western backs up with his National Energy Policy, which he thumped on the table and told Albertans to like or lump. Earlier, Trudeau had sent Gérard Pelletier into the West to sell the policy of biculturalism and bilingualism, and Pelletier had gone about it so clumsily that most Westerners turned hostile and have stayed that way ever since.

From Chrétien, though, they would listen to anything; he had the rare gift of allaying people's suspicions and compelling them to warm to him. It was this quality, more than any other, that he projected in his leadership campaign, and that is why the Chrétien workers were different from the others, feeling a bond to the candidate that did not exist in the other camps.

Without him, there would have been no contest, just a Turner coronation. One version was that the party apparatus ran him to create the illusion of a race, but that he had slipped the leash and come to think he had a real chance.

At the start of the campaign, Marc Lalonde had said the principle of alternation should apply, and Chrétien very nearly quit right there and then. But on March 8, Pierre Trudeau put in a word. Nobody had handed the leadership to him in 1968, when it was the Quebec turn, and he very nearly lost it to Robert Winters. Said Trudeau: "It would be a mistake not to go for the best person, whether he or she be English or French, man or woman, or of some other ethnic stock. I think the Liberals should go for the best person to lead the party."

In Chrétien's mind, there was no doubt that he was that "best person," even though he was shocked by the number of his Quebec cabinet and caucus colleagues flocking to the Turner colours. Chrétien said he was looking in the swimming pool "but I found there was ice on the water because of this so-called principle of alternating."

He dove in, anyway.

Swimming boldly, he turned on reporters for their hailing of Turner, complaining "you elected him without asking him a question."

He said he would be a leader who reflects Main Street, not Bay Street. He said that while Turner had jumped the Liberal ship in 1975, "it is not without great pride that I can say I have served Pierre Elliott Trudeau with loyalty every day since April 4, 1968, through good times and times not so good."

He claimed his budgets as finance minister had been better for the average Canadian than those of John Turner. And yet, if Turner had started the cycle of federal deficits, it was Chrétien who had boosted them into double digits for the first time in Canadian history.

And in 1978, he had been humbled by Trudeau, who went on national television to announce that his government was cutting spending by $2 billion. Trudeau had not confided in Chrétien, his finance minister. But Chrétien hung in, came up with a device called the refundable child tax credit, and brought in a budget with new tax breaks for investors and the middle classes.

Nothing worked, and unemployment mounted along with inflation, contributing to the defeat of the Liberal government in 1979.

When the Liberals returned to power in 1980, Trudeau put Chrétien in justice and entrusted finance to Allan MacEachen, with catastrophic results. Chrétien's time as the first French-speaking finance minister is still the subject of controversy, and gave his critics the basis for their doubts that he could handle the big jobs in government. Could he be prime minister?

A former finance minister, Mitchell Sharp, thought he could, and supported Chrétien's candidacy. Allan Mac-Eachen thought not. So, it seemed, did Marc Lalonde, who replaced MacEachen in the finance portfolio, becoming the second Quebecker ever to hold the job.

Key Quebec Liberals agreed—Labour Minister André Ouellet, Quebec Liberal Caucus Chairman Dennis Dawson, Communications Minister Francis Fox, all flocked to Turner.

Chrétien winced, and soldiered on.

He got a break when Turner said the Manitoba language controversy was a provincial, not a federal issue. Turner issued a clarification, and Chrétien attacked that. And when Turner said he supported Quebec's Bill 101 in principle, Chrétien scoffed, and scoffed again when Turner tried to clarify his position.

And all the while, Chrétien kept repeating his message of unabashed emotional patriotism, and getting standing ovations across the land.

MPs like Pierre Gimaiel, who had doubted Chrétien's leadership potential, came to say that Quebeckers liked Chrétien's style. Yet he preferred Turner, and it was said that Quebec would break Jean Chrétien's heart.

Lise Bissonnette, editor-in-chief of Montreal's *Le Devoir*, said she felt humiliated by Chrétien's line that he was a real peasouper, and jibed that ''English Canada likes him because that's how it wants to see us.'' Chrétien called her a snob who would rather talk to the president of Chad while he would prefer to talk to the little guy in the tavern. Bissonnette came full circle during the campaign when she accused Turner of arrogance.

All through the campaign, there was talk of women's issues, and yet women were little in evidence in an all-male field. Chrétien's lifelong love, his wife Aline, was laid up after an operation for gallstones and could be at his side only occasionally, demonstrating her role as her husband's political sparkplug.

And there were no major roles for Geills Turner, or Heather Johnston, or Dr. Lily Munro, or Elizabeth Whelan, much less the estranged wives of Mark MacGuigan and John Roberts.

It was fascinating that, in an age when equal rights for women counted so much politically, not a single woman was running for the prime ministership, and the wives of the male candidates were all inclined to old-fashioned supportiveness of their men.

Gone was the assertiveness of Maureen McTeer, the most exciting thing about the Joe Clark menage, and yet a political burden in the sense that her image tended to overpower his.

Gone was the incredible Margaret Trudeau with her brand of unstable courage, refusing to be overwhelmed by the self-satisfied, set-in-his-ways man she had married, saying defiantly that she refused to be a rose in her husband's lapel. Before Pierre socked her and sacked her, Margaret did more to bring Canada to the attention of the world than any other person, and as a leftover flower child she at least tried to be true to her convictions, while giving Trudeau the kids he craved to comfort his twilight years.

Now it was the terrible-tempered Geills Turner, tamed somewhat for her role as wife of the prime minister, skilled in the arts of high-born hospitality, a daddy's girl from the rich side of the tracks who had dabbled in thoughts of a career before she married the young MP who would be PM. She can be as testy as Maryon Pearson was, but not as thoughtful, nor as witty. A lot easier on her man, surely, than Mrs. Pearson was.

Aline Chrétien and Jean were sweethearts from the time she was sixteen. Her pretty, dark-eyed-doll face shines out of hundreds of photographs, but there is no record of her having done or said anything of substance politically, at any stage of her husband's long political career. Brothers, sisters, cousins, uncles, aunts, all worked on the Chrétien campaign, to the point where he claimed to have 250 relatives on board. Aline's role was that of the good and loving and faithful wife, and she played it to perfection.

And if fighters for equal rights would lament the "yes, massa" roles of Mrs. Turner and Mme. Chrétien, what would they make of Mila Mulroney?

She, too, was brilliant in her own right, and her intellectual brilliance certainly matches that of her husband. She might even have made a good president of the Iron Ore Company of Canada, and she surely would have made a good MP, a younger Iona Campagnolo in pep, appearance, and personality, with the additional gift of multiple languages and a global way of looking at things. All this, plus an impish sense of humour and a way with women as well as men, dampened only by whatever resentment the sisterhood might have for her trend-setting taste in clothes and household decor.

Yet, Mila Mulroney had chosen the supportive role, backing her husband to the hilt. Her attitude, and that of Geills Turner and Aline Chrétien, might be called a throwback to another time, and yet there had never been a remembered time when Canadian prime ministers had supportive spouses, excepting only the fawning sweetness of Olive Diefenbaker, who came to the job late in life and kept her husband from being driven around the bend by the stresses imposed on him by his fellow Tories.

King and Bennett had never married, though wealthy women showered material benefits upon them. The wife of Louis St. Laurent hated politics and refused to live in Ottawa, preferring sanctuary in the big family home in Quebec. Maryon Pearson regarded her husband's time in politics as "a waste of Mike," and said so to the point where the party regarded her as a ticking time bomb.

And supporters came to feel it would have been better if Pierre Trudeau had never met Margaret, much less married her. And a lot of Tories said the same thing about the match between Clark and McTeer, though of all political wives she was most her own person, and most in tune with her times.

Of all the prime ministers, Pierre Trudeau was the sexiest, and in the business of turning women on, as in so many other aspects of political success, Trudeau would be a hard act to follow.

John Turner, it was said, left women cold for all his good looks. Jean Chrétien, Dalton Camp's nomination for "driver of the getaway car," warmed them up, and reminded some of French actor Jean Paul Belmondo.

Chrétien said he was easygoing and joked about himself, something Trudeau or Turner would never do. That made people comfortable with him, he said, "but others feel that you have to be an imperial type to be prime minister."

Mostly, he talked image and emotion, but occasionally he talked policy. He attacked Turner's proposal to shift the energy emphasis back into Alberta and out of the Beaufort Sea. A longtime supporter of Arctic development, he said drilling must continue wherever there was the possibility of finding oil, if the country was ever to achieve self-sufficiency. He predicted Turner would come to share the Chrétien view, just as he had on Manitoba language rights.

And to those who doubted that Chrétien could be a credit to Canada on the world stage, he said he would establish an anti-nuclear dialogue with other middle powers, following up the Trudeau peace initiative.

He attacked what he called "creeping protectionism" and said he would drive for open markets at home and abroad, pledging that he would be a hard bargainer. One of his objectives would be to have Japanese cars and car parts produced in Western Canada.

"To be competitive abroad," he said, "we must ensure that our own economic union is strong at home—how can we have a strong international presence if provincial governments restrict the movement of goods and workers from one province to another?"

Through it all, he kept saying with a stiff, if slanted, upper lip that he was glad to be second in the lead-up to the convention, "leaving Turner cutting the wind, which he seems to find very difficult."

He attracted a sad assortment of cabinet ministers to

Leadership candidate Donald Johnston was all smiles as he arrived at the Ottawa Civic Centre for the Liberal convention. (UPC/Gary Hershorn)

Leadership candidate Eugene Whelan arrives at the Ottawa Civic Centre with a few of his supporters. (UPC/Nick Didlick)

Leadership candidate Mark MacGuigan waves to supporters as he arrives for a meeting at the Ottawa Civic Centre during the leadership convention. (UPC/Hans Deryk)

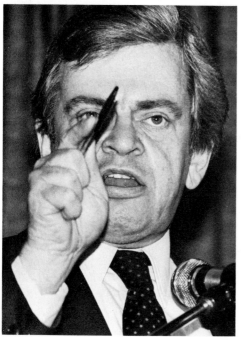

Leadership candidate John Munro uses his pen to make a point as he addresses the youth delegates at the Liberal convention. (UPC/Gary Hershorn)

John Roberts, Liberal leadership hopeful, waves to supporters as he arrives at the Ottawa Civic Centre. (UPC/Gary Hershorn)

Liberal leadership candidate Jean Chrétien is mobbed by people wanting to shake his hand while visiting his hospitality tent in downtown Ottawa. (UPC/Hans Deryk)

Mark MacGuigan (L) moved to the Turner camp after the first vote at the leadership convention. Turner campaign chairman Bill Lee (R) applauds the decision. (UPC/Hans Deryk)

Jean Chrétien wipes his brow after three candidates, (L-R) John Roberts, John Munro and Eugene Whelan, moved to his camp after the first vote. (UPC/Nick Didlick)

Prime Minister Trudeau strikes his famous "gunslinger" pose on stage at the gala evening honouring him as leader of the Liberal party for the past 16 years. (UPC/Nick Didlick)

While his wife Aline looks on, Jean Chrétien thanks the delegates after he lost to John Turner. (UPC/Andy Clark)

Prime Minister-designate John Turner waves his arm in victory following his winning the leadership of the Liberal party. (UPC/Hans Deryk)

Prime Minister-designate John Turner shows he is a man of many faces during a news conference in Ottawa in June. (UPC/Andy Clark)

*Prime Minister Pierre Trudeau
and Prime Minister-designate
John Turner walk to the weekly
Liberal caucus meeting on
Parliament Hill to discuss when
to hold an election. (UPC/Ron
Poling)*

*John Turner and his wife Geills
leave for London to meet with
Queen Elizabeth II and British
Prime Minister Margaret Thatcher.
(UPC/Andy Clark)*

his side—Revenue Minister Pierre Bussières, Multi-culturalism Minister David Collenette, Environment Minister Charles Caccia, Senator Bud Olson, Fisheries Minister Pierre De Bané, and Supply and Services Minister Charles Lapointe—not quite the cream of the weakest cabinet ever. The final flourish came when Public Works Minister Roméo LeBlanc, at the end of his political string, endorsed Chrétien.

Chrétien tried everything. In mid-campaign he said Turner had peaked too soon because the news media "hyped" his candidacy. Chrétien said he knew it was a hype and that it would collapse. But while media adulation of Turner did abate, the Turner campaign kept rolling.

Chrétien called Turner "crazy" on the language issue, and said clarifications wouldn't make for good government.

He promised to be more populist than Trudeau, quicker to make decisions, with more yesses and more no's but not as many maybes.

St. Boniface MP Bob Bockstael, who with Lloyd Axworthy constituted the entire elected caucus of Liberals in the West, endorsed Chrétien, saying he preferred a man who could stick with it and do a job well. But the other half of the elected Western caucus, Lloyd Axworthy, was a cabinet minister with millions in patronage to dispense, and he was running Turner's campaign.

In Quebec, Chrétien swept the convention delegates from the ridings of Pierre Trudeau and Marc Lalonde. But from Trudeau there was no sign of encouragement, despite his hatred for John Turner. And Lalonde was leaning to Turner's side.

Chrétien kept talking. If elected, he said, he would bring in a system of proportional representation for federal elections, to ensure western representation in the federal government.

He promised women equal pay for work of equal value, improved pension provisions and child care services, but rejected quotas "because they tend to be ceilings rather than floors and give the impression of action often without making real change."

Late in the campaign, he put emphasis on how different

he was from Trudeau. "I am a very accessible person," he said in Toronto. "I think Mr. Trudeau was less accessible than I am. I made fifty speeches last year for the party in different parts of the country. I don't think Mr. Trudeau made that many. Decisions would be a lot snappier under me than under Trudeau."

He said many New Democrats supported his bid for the Liberal leadership, causing NDP MP Doug Anguish to deny that Chrétien was referring to him.

When Turner supporters started saying that if the party chose Turner they would get Chrétien, too, he said he didn't want to be Turner's janitor.

He attacked the banks vigorously, saying they were fat, sanctimonious, and full of mistakes.

"An owner of a company," he said, "if he fails, he loses everything, but the banks have no problem. They are the ones who invested in Dome Petroleum. We did not bail out Dome, we bailed out the banks."

There was criticism of Chrétien's preference for one-page briefing memos, and his tendency, in top cabinet jobs, of concentrating on major issues and leaving the details to civil servants.

One of Chrétien's main handlers retorted: "A Chrétien government would be fun—free-wheeling, flexible, partisan, and open. It would have a record of formidable achievements because Chrétien is a conciliator. He can make a deal, he can take a hard situation and bring about a resolution."

Always, in photographs, there was the crooked grin, the product of childhood facial paralysis and partial deafness. There was pride of family, 250 relatives working for this seventeenth of nineteen children. There was his daughter, France, married to the son of Quebec's leading promoter and industrialist, Paul Demarais. And his adopted son, Michel, an Indian.

Through it all, Chrétien had never left Shawinigan, forty kilometres up his beloved St. Maurice River from Trois Rivières. That river provided the power for the industries that gathered there.

It was in one of those paper mills, now owned by Consolidated Bathurst, that Chrétien's father, Willie, worked for fifty years, raising the survivors of his nineteen children.

Each of the boys got a summer job in the mill, and each found an escape route from the drudgery their father and mother knew. The eldest son, Maurice, was finished medical school by the time the three youngest, Guy, Jean, and Michel, were taking their first lessons.

Mama Chrétien worked out a deal with the priests at the Joliette seminary, giving tuition for three at the price of two.

Chrétien recalls that he was a terrible kid, and that his mother dreaded showing his report cards to his father. ''I just couldn't accept rules,'' he recalls. The crooked mouth brought taunts from his schoolmates, and got him into a lot of fights.

That's where he learned about street fighting, he says, recalling one bully who was going to pound him: ''I tell him I don't want to fight. He gets closer. I say my ankle is hurt and I can't fight. He comes right up to me with his guard down. So I hit him and lay him out.''

Asked why he chose federal rather than provincial politics at a time when Quebec nationalism was starting to boil, Chrétien tells of a discussion he was having about separatists in the federal public service, and how he was blaming things on *les Anglais*. Another young lawyer said Chrétien had no knowledge of the English and didn't know what he was talking about. So Chrétien decided to go to Ottawa and find out.

The first step was fighting Social Credit, in whose philosophy Chrétien disbelieved completely. After he won the St. Maurice seat from the Créditistes, he kept campaigning against them until the movement died out completely—whereupon he turned his energies in Quebec to fighting separatists, a battle that he feels has gone well, but one that may never end.

Altogether, a totally absorbing and interesting guy, with a quick wit and a quick way with words. For those of us in media, Chrétien times would indeed have been fun times, a stimulating carry-over from the frantic Trudeau years. And that slanted us in his favour—at least, it did me.

When Turner and Trudeau clashed over the background to Turner's quitting the cabinet in disgust in 1975, Chrétien supported Trudeau's view, as expressed by the prime minister in an unusually testy press release. But Trudeau and Turner agreed to bury the hatchet and the incident came to nothing, with the public and the rest of us no wiser about the reason for Turner's defection than we were when it happened.

Chrétien said he would expand mortgage rate insurance to farmers and other businessmen if it worked well with homeowners.

In Edmonton, Turner supporter Chester Tanner called Chrétien "Mr. Chargex"—"because he takes credit for everything."

Said Chrétien: "People say I have no depth because my words are always simple. But to make everything simple, you have to understand all the intricacies of a problem. Otherwise you mess it up."

He had never messed it up, and never dropped the ball.

"I'm a tough bugger," he told one campaign audience. "You would like me to give you a profound dissertation on the philosophy that motivates me, and I won't."

At campaign's end, he returned to Shawinigan, recalling previous heroes of the St. Maurice valley, the explorers Radisson, Groseilliers, La Vérendrye. Petit Jean would paddle his canoe down the St. Maurice, and upto Ottawa and 24 Sussex Drive.

"I knew when I came in," he said, "that I didn't have more than 25 per cent chance of winning. Now I have 50." Whenever the party needed someone, he said, they could always count on Jean. Good old reliable Jean.

When Quebec delegates were in the voting booth, he told reporters, they would be alone with their hearts and their consciences.

In the event, most of them voted for Turner, and Pierre Trudeau cast his ballot for Donald Johnston.

10

BLUE EYES

Turner went up to the attic,
Nursing those leadership blues
When he comes out of seclusion
He'll look just like old Howard Hughes.
Beautiful, beautiful blue eyes,
Gleaming like jewels, those two eyes
Leading those don't-have-a-clue guys,
Who'll learn to love Turner again.
Parody, January, 1984 (acknowledgment to D. Crombie).

The Liberals had always believed that they governed Canada by Divine Right, so it was appropriate that God sent them John Turner when they needed him. If He hadn't, they would have had to invent him, which some people think they did.

Actually, it was a re-invention, dusting off from retirement a man from the party's past and plonking him squarely in the middle of the 1980s.

And having re-invented Turner, they charged him with the job of re-inventing the Liberal Party itself, ensuring that federal power would remain with the anointed party to the turn of the century and beyond.

It was potent stuff—as potent, in its way, as the invention of Pierre Elliott Trudeau in 1968, and the second coming of Trudeau in 1980. Then, as now, it would be a triumph of personality over policy, of image over substance. Turner would be sold as the man with the winning way, the way Robert Stanfield's backers sold him to the Conservative Party in 1967.

The difference was that if Turner made it to the Liberal leadership, he would pick up the prime ministership along with it, and possession of power was the name of the Liberal game.

There would be obstacles to overcome.

Trudeau's distaste for Turner, returned in kind, was one.

Turner's walkout on the party in 1975 was another.

Then there was Turner's boardroom manner, picked up in nine years among the business elite. To go with that was the chequered history of some of Turner's business ventures.

And the man was macho in an age when feminine qualities were in fashion. He was, to some, a better Tory than he was a Grit.

He hadn't made a political speech, nor granted a political interview, in all the years away. He had issued occasional newsletters critical of Trudeau policies, and especially critical of the man who would be his main opponent for the leadership, Jean Chrétien.

None of these things, his advisers told him, would matter a damn. The party was in trouble and only he could turn things around, because he was a turnaround kind of guy. The biggest problem, in fact, would be to avoid the impression of a coronation, which would cost the party the hoped-for convention momentum, and make him vulnerable to his ultimate opponent, Brian Mulroney.

So the carefully crafted, long-contemplated Turner campaign was put in place, and he entered the campaign the front runner, after two weeks of preparatory contemplation. There was as little doubt that he would come in, as there was that he would win.

At his opening press conference in Ottawa on March 16, he said many people had wondered why he would give up a secure and comfortable life for the risks of politics. His answer was that it was a way he could give back to his country a small measure of what it had given to him.

The fact was that not many people had wondered, and that most felt he wanted to be prime minister, that he craved the thing the Liberals wanted most, power. He always had, and that was one of the reasons he resented Trudeau staying so long, and wanting to stay longer, thus carrying Turner beyond his destined time.

Now, for Turner, everything was coming up roses, and he promised openness, accessibility, and accountability of government.

Yet he started by running on his previous record in politics, and refusing to accept questions about that record, and about the reasons for his sudden retirement in 1975. Instead, he put himself forward as the man of the future, the antidote to the Trudeau years, the great conciliator and achiever.

At the start of the campaign, he seemed to be paying a price for his years out of politics. His statements about language rights being provincial brought howls from minorities in Manitoba and Quebec, and he took refuge in clarifications and reminders that he had been a prime promoter of the Official Languages Act. When the smoke cleared, as it did, he had appealed to redneck elements in the West and in Quebec, without ever coming right out with it.

In the process, he had put Brian Mulroney at risk with the Tory western majority, a good weapon for the election to come in which Turner would be shooting for a Liberal revival in the West.

And when he put out a version of his 1975 split with Trudeau, it fetched a testy response from Trudeau himself, and the two agreed to disagree after Turner apologized, saying he had thought he was talking off the record to reporters on a bus. But the incident put distance between himself and Trudeau, one of the prime objects of the Turner campaign.

There remained the problem of Turner's business acumen, and the failure of some of his Bay Street promotions. These, too, were swept aside by him as unimportant, and the issue came to nothing.

That left only Jean Chrétien to be disposed of— Chrétien the campaigner, catching fire with delegates and with Canadians generally, but bucking what turned out to be a fatal obstacle: the perception of Turner as a winner, and the conviction that sixteen years of leadership by a French Canadian was enough. It was a conviction that large numbers of Quebeckers shared, denying Chrétien the solid home-province support he would need to beat Turner. Chrétien's record of political accomplishment during the years when Turner was away could be attacked on the ground that Chrétien was all emotion and that he lacked stability.

The early rough spots in the Turner campaign did take some of the starry-eyed adulation out of media coverage, and the things that were said and written about Turner turned increasingly critical.

Turner's prime backer in Quebec, Labour Minister André Ouellet, said it wasn't fair, as if fairness had a place in elections or leadership campaigns. In the end, it didn't matter. Nobody in media pursued the loose ends in the Turner story, because events were moving too fast.

At least, they seemed to be moving too fast; in fact, nothing important was moving at all, and the action was illusory, sustained by all-candidate meetings at five points around the country that drew maximum media attention. The real work was going on not among the electorate, but among the 3,500-odd convention delegates who would make the decision. More than 1,000 of them were ex-officio members of the party apparatus, and the basis for Turner's strength was there.

Nobody, not even a corporation lawyer, could come out of years in business with an unblemished record of success, and with Turner the blemish was a firm called Infinitum Growth Fund Inc., peddled under his name in early 1980 to take advantage of an Ontario subsidy for high-risk industrial ventures. The businesses involved included film-making, plastic mouldings, hospital supplies, and hockey sticks. Nothing sold. As Turner said, "some situations work well, some less well." Brief fuss, end of story, except for investors left holding the bag. Hell, it was high risk money, anyway—they had as good a fling as they would have had in Las Vegas.

There was one other minor tremor, the report of tax troubles for Sandoz Canada Inc., the big chemical multinational of which Turner was a director. That firm makes NeoCitran among a myriad of other things, so people might identify with it. But Turner dismissed the affair as peanuts—all big firms negotiate with Revenue Canada all the time. Next question.

What about Turner's directorships?

What about them, responded Turner, a fellow has to make a living and there's the wife and kids to think of. He kept his directorships throughout the leadership campaign, and even renewed two of them—Canadian Pacific and Seagram—in the month before the convention. His directors' fees were more than $100,000 a year, and there would be time enough to resign when the prime minister-ship was his.

It could be, of course, that his directorships helped him in politics, representing a measure of achievement. Against that was the suspicion that companies wanted him on the board because of his political record and his prospects of becoming prime minister. It was a question that would never be resolved, and not much was made of it, nor did we ever hear whether Turner was an effective member of all those boards, or just a glossy item in the annual reports. By the time anybody got around to asking, most of the people with the answer were on the Turner bandwagon and at least one of them, Canadian Pacific's Ian Sinclair, was in the Senate, put there not by Turner, but by Trudeau.

Lloyd Axworthy, who would have run for the leadership in 1979 had Trudeau not changed his mind, signed on as Turner's national campaign co-chairman, after agonizing over whether to enter the contest himself. He cited personal considerations for his decision not to run, one of which was love for his second wife, his first marriage having blown up. His best option, said skilled politician Axworthy, was "to go with a guy who I think can win the next election."

The Turner campaign was just as cold-blooded as that, which is why so much of the appeal shifted to Jean Chrétien, the guy everybody came to love but few thought could win. It became known as the "head vs. heart" campaign, and "head" stayed out in front all the way.

After the Manitoba language hassle, the *Ottawa Citizen* wrote:

> Turner's first week in the race has not been notably
> successful. A front runner who falters so early risks having
> a cloud over his whole campaign. There is equal confusion to
> be drawn from his generalities on the economy, and his
> apparent views of the nature of Confederation. Is he in
> favour of decentralized government? How will he improve
> the economy and reduce the deficit?

Who cared? The questions were never answered, because they did not need to be. By the end of the campaign Turner was talking less about cutting the horrendous federal deficit than he had at the beginning, but the impression was clear: if he won a full mandate in an election, a painful attack on the deficit would be his first priority, just as it was for the Tories in 1979 and would be again if Brian Mulroney came to power. But you wouldn't win elections or leaderships on that.

Mulroney jibed at Turner's claim to be the candidate of experience, saying: "If by experience you mean declaring your candidacy on a Friday, disavowing positions in regard to protection of minority rights on Saturday, repudiating decades of Liberal policy by Monday, reversing yourself by Tuesday and swallowing yourself whole by Thursday—if that is experience, then I'll have none of it."

But Mulroney didn't have a vote, though by campaign's end the Conservatives were putting out the story that they would rather face Turner in an election than take on Chrétien.

News coverage of the early weeks of the Liberal leadership campaign swung slowly over to Chrétien, who was getting standing ovations all over the country with his appeals to patriotism and his shouts that "Canada is Number One!"

And there was a boom for Liberal President Iona Campagnolo, reaching such a pitch in some quarters that it was said she could have the leadership for the asking. Fortunately for her, Mrs. Campagnolo knew better, so she took the accolades for what they were worth and got on with her work of organizing the convention.

"I'm very flattered," she told delegates at a Toronto meeting, "but you simply have to stop doing this." Eventually, they did, and "draft Iona" buttons became the curios of the campaign, replaced by the tiny "Iona" pins she herself produced as tokens of her re-election, by acclamation, as party president.

Occasionally, Turner put some juice into his campaigning. At his alma mater, the University of British Columbia, he pulled on an athletic sweater, reminiscent of his days as a track star, his springboard for a Rhodes Scholarship in the mold portrayed by Robert Taylor in the 1930s' film *A Yank at Oxford*.

"If I can achieve anything on your behalf," he told cheering students, "I would like you to be able to dream again the way my generation dreamed."

Was he too far from the people? No, said he. In Calgary, he said this: "If there is anything I know, it is how to get along with other human beings. There is not a city or a town in any part of Canada that I haven't had the good fortune to walk down and within five minutes know someone by their first name."

Yet one headline proclaimed that "failure to generate enthusiasm could be Turner's Achilles' heel."

And an endless succession of biographies in print speculated that, like Trudeau, he was a naturally shy man who had assumed an activist personality as a cover-up, that he was nervous with people and press, that he was running on his reflexes, and that they were the reflexes of another age.

One of the few funny stories from the Turner campaign came from Thunder Bay, where a reporter sought a dinner-time interview so she could get away to interview singer Engelbert Humperdinck, who was in the same motel. Turner was piqued, and said: "She's got her priorities all wrong—she had to meet some guy called Humperdinckle."

"The delegates," said Turner, "are looking for leadership. I feel I'm responding the way they expect me to."

In Quebec, the Turner apparatus kept picking up delegates, sucking the lifeblood out of the Chrétien candidacy. Dennis Dawson, the Liberal MP for Louis-Hébert and president of the Quebec caucus, said the support of key Quebec ministers was a big factor—"People like Francis Fox and André Ouellet have their structures of power." And Shefford MP Jean Lapierre said: "Liberals here are not only members of a party. They belong to a government. Let's face it. We've been in power for forty-three out of the last fifty years. And these people want to stay in power."

Au revoir, M. Chrétien.

As the campaign unfolded, Turner did get to talk a bit about policy, though always in generalities.

In Saskatoon, he said, "There are a lot of projects over the past number of years, without being too specific, we could have done without. We'll certainly be specific about the future but I'm not going to be specific about the past."

In Winnipeg, on April 4, Turner unveiled a phrase he would use in his convention victory speech: "Mr. Trudeau is the most remarkable Canadian of his generation." But, as he would at the convention, he went on to say that the biggest task facing Trudeau's successor was rebuilding the Liberals as a national party.

When Tories talk like that, people laugh, but when Liberals do it, people listen. In the western provinces, Liberal Party memberships were going up, reflected in the public opinion polls. In the Bow River riding association, Vice-president Randy Royer said, "The biggest thing that's drawing in people is John Turner and nobody else."

In Toronto, Turner pledged that, once in office, he would curb the influence of the political fixers who had dominated Ottawa under Trudeau. He said it was for the legislature and government of Ontario to decide whether or not the province should be declared bilingual. Ontario Liberals responded by giving Turner the lion's share of their convention delegates.

By mid-campaign, Turner was talking more about jobs than he was about the deficit.

Jobs would be his first priority, restoring confidence in the Canadian economy and encouraging risk-takers. And he would follow policies in the interests of "the new majority, women". That would include equal pay for work of equal value in sectors within federal jurisdiction. His coaches on the gender issue were cabinet minister Judy Erola and Monique Bégin, and they let it be known that Turner was a quick learner, with a lot to learn. Rumour had it that it took him more than a day to get his tongue around the "equal pay for work of equal value" pledge, but he learned not only to say it with conviction but to believe it himself.

In Newfoundland, he said the province should be entitled to the majority of offshore oil revenues, and pledged that Newfoundlanders would get first call on offshore jobs. Newfoundland delegates scoffed and went heavily for Chrétien.

"Where have you been the last eight years?" asked a heckler in Prince Edward Island.

"I'm not the only person who should be asked that question," replied Turner. "Mulroney wasn't actively present during the last ten years either."

In St. Catharines, he pledged that a Turner government "will do nothing behind closed doors—I want a party that is open, visible, and public, a government of consultation and consensus and not a government of confrontation and ultimatum."

In Winnipeg, he presented an eight-point agenda for the West, but again it was short on specifics. When he said "I know your sense of frustration and alienation," the Manitoba audience gave him a standing ovation.

And the polls continued to show him ahead, but with

Chrétien creeping up. The rest of the field of candidates dragged hopelessly behind, and as long as they continued to do so, Turner's handlers were happy. They talked of a first-ballot win.

In the last week of April, Turner brought in Bill Lee to be director of his campaign organization. This was the same Bill Lee who had helped Paul Hellyer unify the armed forces during the Pearson years, following which he organized Hellyer's disastrous run for the Liberal leadership against Trudeau in 1968. When Trudeau won, he hired Lee to travel with him during the Trudeaumania election, following which Lee started his own business, using prime ministerial letterhead. Of Lee it was said that he knows it all. He doesn't, but he knows a lot, and he certainly steadied the Turner team in the final coast to victory.

In Halifax, on May 7, Mark MacGuigan said Turner's plans to cut the federal deficit could only cause widespread suffering, adding: "Canadians don't want Reaganomics, whether it's offered by Tories or Liberals."

And when Don Johnston demanded that delegates be given more than the "vapid generalities" of his rivals, Jean Chrétien responded by saying that Johnston should know a leadership campaign was not a time for spelling out detailed policy, but a time for showing the personalities and strengths of the candidates.

In Ottawa, on May 9, Turner said government must not do anything that would interfere in the competitive jungle of free enterprise. Stagnating firms must be allowed to wither and die, and new businesses must be given full scope to muscle out weak companies.

"Investment is necessary for expansion," he said, "and expansion is necessary for growth, as growth is necessary for jobs." Then he added that the government must provide a safety net for those who are unemployed, ill, aged, or disadvantaged. And he tacked on his pledge about equal pay for work of equal value.

He would conduct an urgent investigation into the affairs of Canadair and de Havilland, the big, government-owned losers in the aerospace industry, but he would not sell off Air Canada, a winner.

In Chambly, Quebec, on May 18, he said he would want Jean Chrétien in his cabinet, because he wanted the strongest government possible "and Quebeckers would want to know they'll have a strong voice in that government."

That same day, in Moncton, Chrétien was attacking Turner for criticizing Trudeau, saying such criticism was against the traditions of the Liberal Party and "Liberals are not known for shooting their leaders, at least while they are still living."

In Montreal, Turner was telling an audience of Italian Canadians that he was a tactile politician, dealing with people "*mano a mano*, eyeball to eyeball, hand to hand."

In Ottawa, on May 24, a survey by *The Canadian Press* showed that a big majority of Liberal senators would back Turner.

Biographies kept emphasizing the role in Turner's life of his mother, Phyllis, and sister Brenda said: "People say Mummy was ambitious. She wasn't particularly, but she...it was a striving for excellence. She knew John was bright and she always expected it of us. And it wasn't a pushing. It wasn't that kind of ambition. It was just that if you've been given talents, given gifts, use them."

Shades of Pierre Trudeau's mother, and John Diefenbaker's, and Joe Clark's, and Louis St. Laurent's, and Willie King's, not to mention Winston Churchill's and Franklin D. Roosevelt's and John F. Kennedy's and Jimmy Carter's. Talk about women as the "new majority"! Mother Mulroney. Or Mama Chrétien, bringing up nine highly-motivated children in a Quebec mill town, while mourning the ten infants who died.

Contemplate, for a moment, the influence of the two Mrs. Turners, Phyllis and Geills, mother and wife of John. And keep in mind the strain of his knowing that his once so vibrant mother lies suffering from Alzheimer's Disease in a nursing home on B.C.'s Salt Spring Island, and that when he visits her she doesn't recognize him, nor can she know that he has realized her grandest ambition for him.

Phyllis Turner became a *grande dame*, but she did it in the British Columbia frontier fashion, growing up in Rossland, B.C., with her sisters Marcella and Gladys, daughters of James Gregory, a hoistman at the Centre Star and Le Roi gold mines above the town.

Marcella and Gladys grew up to be schoolteachers in the Kootenays. Phyllis became the church organist before following a scholarship trail that led her to Eastern Canada, the United States, and England.

People remember her from those days as much for her beauty as for her brains. In England, while studying at the London School of Economics, she met and married a young gadabout adventurer and journalist named Leonard Hugh Turner, who wrote for the *Manchester Guardian* and freelanced for *Punch* magazine.

They had three children: John, Michael, and Brenda. Michael choked to death in hospital for lack of proper post-natal care, though he had been as robust at birth as older brother John. John inherited his father's good looks, if not his gentle nature, and was just two years old when Leonard Turner died, at age twenty-nine of hyperthyroidism.

Lacking any personal recollection of his father, Turner picked up bits and pieces of lore from his father's brother, Will, who lives in East Sussex, having made the connection with his uncle during the years at Oxford. Will spun Turner some tall tales about his father, telling him that Leonard had been a roustabout in Java, and that he got malaria in Sumatra, and had a brief career as a gunsmith in that Somerset Maugham setting.

After her husband's death, Phyllis came back to Rossland, staying there for two years, thus enabling her son to claim the place as one of his many home towns: his birthplace Richmond in England, then Rossland, then Vancouver, Montreal, Ottawa, and Toronto. It was not the least of the many things Phyllis Turner did for John. Says sister Brenda: "John went to camp every summer because he had no father, and mummy wanted to make sure." He went to Ottawa's elite Ashbury College for polish, and then to St. Pat's College where he learned to fight and had Roman Catholicism drilled into his bones to the point where he once contemplated the priesthood. (To this day, he ranks the two top callings in the world as religion and politics, in that order, and his devout Catholicism is much remarked upon, though wife Geills is Anglican and the Turner sons go to Protestant Upper Canada College.)

Leaving Rossland, Mrs. Turner headed for Ottawa and the beginnings of a remarkable career in government and high society.

She got a job as an economist with the tariff board in Ottawa, and, when war came, she parlayed her talents and connections into the job of federal administrator of oils and fats, including candy bars and paints. She was a woman of achievement in a world full of men—what is more, men of a higher calibre than have been drawn into public service since. This was the wonder world of C. D. Howe and his dollar-a-year men, so many of whom became the prime movers and shapers of post-war industrial Canada.

Phyllis Turner held court in her own household, entertaining the great and near-great of the time, one of whom was a Montreal/Vancouver millionaire named Frank Ross, who made his money banking, shipbuilding, and dredging. John was sixteen when his mother married Ross at the end of the war.

Ross had connections in business and in the Liberal Party. When the family headed west it was a chance for John Turner to go to the University of British Columbia, where he blossomed as an athlete and scholar, winning his Rhodes and getting himself back to the land of his birth.

Turner has always objected to stories that he grew up with a silver spoon in his mouth, noting that he, like his mother, had had to work his own way through life, and protesting that he never did earn any serious money until he quit politics for Bay Street.

But interviews with his old fellow scholars at Magdalen College, Oxford, create a picture of a rich young man dining on imported steak (he insists it was cans of corned beef) and driving fast cars in an England where rationing was still strictly enforced. Turner had lots of style, made plenty of friends, got his degrees, and went off for a year at the University of Paris.

If his father was like a Somerset Maugham character,

Turner the student stands out in people's minds as somebody out of Scott Fitzgerald, full of energy, determined to do the proper thing, yet wanting to be one of the boys.

He recalls celebrating his twenty-first birthday in Oscar Wilde's old college rooms, with twenty-one male friends all clad in rented dinner jackets. Not just any friends—men who would matter, as Turner would. Roger Bannister and Chris Chataway were there, the great runners and Turner's track teammates; Malcolm Fraser, a future prime minister of Australia; Kenneth Tynan, critic and author and future husband of Matthew Halton's daughter, Kathleen; and Walter Clements, the American writer. Turner not only wined and dined with them, he made them part of the Turner network, at least in his own mind.

Mother kept the food and money coming, along with advice and introductions, and in the meantime she herself was cutting a wide swath in Vancouver society, where people came to regard her almost with awe. In 1955, Frank Ross was appointed lieutenant-governor of British Columbia by Prime Minister Lester Pearson—and Pearson was already eyeing John Turner as a future Liberal politician.

Ross caused the government of British Columbia to build a grand new Victoria residence for its lieutenant-governor, but before it was ready he and Phyllis entertained Princess Margaret, then the glamour girl of the royal family, making her first tour of Canada.

Turner, by this time, was embarked on his legal career in Montreal and, at first, he declined his mother's invitation to attend the Vancouver festivities for the princess.

Sister Brenda: ''He just didn't want any part of stepfather's being Lieutenant-Governor. He was setting out as a young lawyer in Montreal, he wanted to make his name on his own, without help from anybody.''

But Brenda persuaded John to go for mother's sake, and so he met the princess, and they danced all night, and the rumours flew of romance, and John Turner's name got into the papers, world-wide.

When Margaret travelled to Ottawa, John Turner appeared again and there were reports of a tryst at the prime ministerial country residence, Harrington Lake. But marauding reporters cluttered up the scene and if there ever was romance, it faded in the bright glare of the publicity.

The story was to follow Turner for years, upto and including his marriage to Geills Kilgour in 1963, by which time he was a Liberal member of parliament, the Liberals having won power from the Diefenbaker Conservatives.

Turner became parliamentary secretary to Arthur Laing, the northern affairs minister, and I can recall visiting Whitehorse on a Laing junket, one of the party being Claude Jodoin, a man of enormous girth who was president of the Canadian Labour Congress.

There was a mass meeting of Whitehorse citizens and the members of the official party spoke. I was sitting beside two of the belles of Whitehorse and when Turner's name was mentioned I told them to get a good hold on themselves because this was the sexiest man in Canada, the prince who had danced with the princess.

When Turner finished speaking I asked if they had felt anything, and both said nothing. Zilch. Not a tremor.

Then Jodoin was announced and waddled up to the platform.

In the midst of his speech, I glanced at my two companions and saw that both had drops of perspiration on the tips of their noses, and beads of sweat were standing out on their foreheads, while their bosoms were heaving. When he finished, both said: ''Now, THERE's a man!''

As for Geills Kilgour, it's never been clear how she reacted to the romantic stories of her husband's youth, because to tell the truth it's never been clear how she reacted to anything, except for her distaste at Turner being Number Two to Trudeau for so long. Even there, the evidence is contradictory—my own impression was that she couldn't stand Margaret Trudeau, whereas others say she was sympathetic and friendly-disposed.

But by no stretch could she be described as one of those women who shaped her husband's career, though she may have been the decisive influence in persuading him to quit politics in 1975 and get some serious money into the family coffers.

She has rightly been described as a very private person

with a quick temper and an impatience with people she perceives to be fools or intruders.

In Turner's previous political incarnation, she frequently attended sessions of the House of Commons, and was always there when he was scheduled to speak, unless she was off having one of their four children.

During the Liberal leadership campaign, Geills Turner went public as she never had before, either for John or for her brother, David, who is the Conservative member of parliament for Edmonton-Strathcona. Like Geills, he is the very properly brought up child of millionaire David Kilgour. And like brother-in-law John, he perfected his French at the University of Paris.

Geills Turner could be counted on to bring the touch of class that has been lacking at 24 Sussex, because she is to the manor bred, and she polished her skills as hostess during the years when social Toronto lionized the Turners.

In one campaign interview, Geills Turner described herself as a Type A personality—a demanding, compulsive perfectionist prone to heart attacks.

Geills Turner likes to win, and she likes her husband to win. In the battle between John Turner and Brian Mulroney, you could not take your eyes off wives Geills and Mila, both of whom are totally involved in their husband's careers and both of whom hate to lose. Geills Turner cares about women's issues, but not with the same gut passion as her husband's mentors on gender politics, Judy Erola and Monique Bégin.

But Turner is by nature a macho man, keeping in mind that his idols include Sir John A. Macdonald, Sir Wilfrid Laurier, Clarence Decatur Howe, Montreal Mayor Jean Drapeau, former Quebec Premier Daniel Johnson (referred to by Turner as Danny Boy), and a host of athletes, with whom he can subside into his comfortable locker room stance, or used to be able to before women gained locker room access.

Back to the campaign.

In Thunder Bay, Turner pledged that he would serve in Opposition as Liberal leader even if his party did not win the next federal election. Few could imagine him doing that, nor could they see Geills acquiescing.

Asked in Sault Ste. Marie if he would serve as an ordinary MP if he lost the leadership bid, he said he believed his experience entitled him to something more. He called himself the recycled man, admitted he had taken a few shots from his rival candidates, but insisted he was happy to be back in the game.

At the start of the campaign, he had referred to politics as a high calling and an honourable career, saying: "It is the duty of all of us to engage in politics, and I include the media as an essential ingredient of that, to seek the highest degree of excellence and integrity." To veteran reporters, it was a far cry from sixteen years ago, when Pierre Trudeau had called us "the crummy press," and threatened to put his police onto our private lives if we kept writing about his.

Turner said his wilderness canoe trips each year with his family had taught him how precious nature is. He pledged to work out a clean air pact with the United States.

The mention of canoe trips called Trudeau to mind, and the story about Craig Oliver, the CTV telecaster who has led many a canoe safari through the northern wilderness, sometimes with Pierre Trudeau aboard. According to this tale, John Turner had asked Oliver for his charts of an Arctic river, showing the hazards and the portages, including one giant waterfall. Oliver told Trudeau of Turner's request, and Trudeau wondered, doubtless in jest, if it would be possible to delete the waterfall from the chart, leaving Turner to his fate.

Oliver's lips are sealed, and Trudeau is saving his best stuff for his own books, so we may never know. Oliver left the charts unaltered, and the Turners navigated the river without mishap.

Back in the campaign, the other candidates were getting more and more personal in their attacks on the front runner, as the convention neared.

Eugene Whelan scoffed at the gold-tinted windows of the Royal Bank Tower, housing Turner's law offices. "Gold flakes in the windows," he said, "when many don't have cornflakes in the plate."

Don Johnston scorned programs that would "return the country to a better yesterday." And referring to the party's power brokers and vested interests (many of whom were backing Turner), he promised to "yank their noses out of the trough." A stimulating image to those of us who once had tried to popularize the phrase "trough Grits" as a counter to the commonplace "rabid Tories."

On June 5, the Toronto *Globe and Mail* reported a survey of delegates showing Turner maintaining his substantial lead, though he had slipped from 54 to 51 per cent, with Chrétien edging from 31 per cent to 32. In Toronto, Turner had 41 per cent of delegates, to Chrétien's 24 per cent.

When an ethnic reporter came to interview him, the tactile Turner threw his arm around the man's shoulder and said the leadership was just phase one of the campaign—the election would be next. "Profit will not be a dirty word," he pledged.

A week before the convention, Turner gave his last public speech and turned his attention to campaign housekeeping, some tennis, and the writing of his victory speech, one of the few "impromptu" orations ever to be bound, in advance, in Moroccan leather.

The closing polls kept saying Turner was the candidate most likely to win an election for the Liberals. Reporters wrote that Turner "almost seemed at ease," and that he had muted his nervous little cough between sentences, though he still smacked his lips with the cricket-like "click" that drove soundmen and tape editors to distraction.

And finally, it was convention time, four days in Ottawa when candidates would blow the final third of their campaign budgets. Into the hoopla moved the Turner entourage, occupying the storied Château Laurier, known irreverently as Disneyland North. The hotel was as much a part of the nation's political history as Parliament Hill

itself—it had housed policy conventions galore, including a
Liberal conclave two years previously at which Turner had
emerged from the woodwork and done a royal-style walk-
about, creating a sensation wherever he went with his
media followers, and disrupting the business in every hall
he entered. For Turner, it was a case of contributing
nothing, but gaining much.

This was the hotel in which Trudeau had welcomed
Liberals to the 1980s on victory night. It was the place
where the Tories had begun the open impeachment of John
Diefenbaker, who had pledged to lay himself down and
bleed awhile, then to rise and fight again.

Here the Liberals, years before, had hailed Bryce
Mackasey as the popular hero of the first Trudeau cabinet,
the self-styled Babe Ruth of strike-solving in his job as
minister of labour.

Here John Bracken, the leader whose sole claim to
fame was that he put the word ''Progressive'' into the
nameplate of the Conservatives, received the only standing
ovation of his time in Ottawa, not realizing that the Eddy
woodpile across the river had caught fire, and that the
audience was rising to get a better view of the flames
visible through the ballroom windows at Bracken's back.

Now, the grand old pile was headquarters to the Turner
camp, while the other candidates spread themselves
around the newer hostelries that, along with the hockey
rink down in Lansdowne Park, sustained Ottawa's claim to
hosting political conventions, against the anguished con-
tentions of Montreal, Toronto, Winnipeg, and Edmonton.

11

BYTOWN REVISITED

The Tories had ventured outside Ottawa for two leadership conventions—1942 in Winnipeg, and 1967 in Toronto—but neither of those conventions produced a prime minister, both Bracken and Robert Stanfield falling short.

In Ottawa, the Conservatives had chosen George Drew, who didn't make it to power, and John Diefenbaker and Joe Clark, who did. And in 1983, they had taken the prize away from Clark and given it to Brian Mulroney, in one of the most dramatic conventions ever.

The Liberals had met in Ottawa to choose Mackenzie King in 1919, and he went on to become the longest ruling prime minister in the history not only of Canada, but of what used to be called the Commonwealth and Empire.

In the same Lansdowne Park cowbarn where the Tories had picked Drew, the Grits chose Louis St. Laurent, the last courtly prime minister, and some said the last gentleman to hold power in Canada.

It was on that same site that the Tories chose John Diefenbaker, and it was there that Lester Pearson was voted Liberal leader, at a time when it seemed the party would be out of office for as far ahead as anybody could see.

Pearson was the beneficiary of Diefenbaker's self-inflicted wounds and enjoyed a stormy five years in office, and when it was time to pick his successor the convention was held in the new rink at Lansdowne Park, known as the Civic Centre.

It was in that arena that Pierre Trudeau was chosen, the starting point for the mania that led him to his quick election victory.

It was there that Joe Clark achieved his astonishing victory in 1976.

But when Trudeau announced his retirement in 1979, the Liberals, writhing in opposition, decided to change their luck and hold their leadership convention in Winnipeg, where a spanking new convention centre had been built to receive them.

It became the convention that never was, because Trudeau reversed himself, and the Winnipeg Convention Centre is still suffering from the loss. In vain did Winnipeg plead its case when Trudeau signalled a leadership convention in 1984. Equally futile was the bid of Edmonton, whose new convention centre was one of the wonders of the burgeoning West.

Ottawa it would be, and Lansdowne Park, and the outside chance of a renewal of party fortunes to match the one engineered in those same precincts by Trudeau sixteen years before.

For Ottawa, the "fat city" that had ridden out the recession on the backs of the nation's taxpayers, it was the icing on the cake: hosting two national political conventions in two successive years was like having the run of the Mint, a licence to print money.

It wasn't just the money—there was also the joy. The people of Ottawa, especially the young people, knew how to enjoy a political convention. The candidates for leadership would have their eyes on convention delegates, but in courting their votes they would set up three nights of revelry that would benefit everybody who cared to turn out, and Ottawa youth turned out in droves.

Middle-aged delegates might have to plug their ears against the assaults of the rock bands, the punk rock singers, the blaring music for the break dancers, but the kids of Ottawa loved it, and covered themselves with pins and badges showing the faces of men the wearers had never heard of.

Parking lots were covered by huge marquees, streets were blocked off, chip wagons ran out of potatoes, and enough hot dogs were sold to stretch from Bonavista to Vancouver Island.

The delegates themselves were more reserved than the Tories had been the year before, telling themselves they had more to be sombre about. After all, they were here to choose a prime minister. And after all, most of them had come with their minds made up—their selection was widely, and correctly, said to have been pre-ordained.

The best fun, because it was the most spontaneous, was in the big Chrétien tent in the heart of the city. The excitement sustained the thought that Chrétien had a chance, a notion that I myself had espoused from the start of the campaign, winning me so much grateful attention from Chrétien supporters that I could not go among them without being cheered, and chaired. It was a lonely place for a media pundit, and it would be even lonelier for Chrétien before the week was out.

There was frantic talk of deals among the back-running candidates, and rumours of an "anybody but Turner" cabal, but it was all talk, all rumours, and in the end it amounted to nothing. In part, it was media manipulation by the backroom schemers, but mostly it was media manipulating itself, creating the illusion of a contest to match those of previous Tory conventions, and the Trudeau sensation of 1968.

The first order of convention business was to say goodbye to Trudeau himself, and for this, the Liberal showmen pulled out all the stops, some of which came off in their hands. For one night, the Ottawa Civic Centre would become Hollywood-on-the-Rideau, and they would bury Trudeau in schlock until he rescued himself, and the evening, with one of the best speeches of his life.

12

GOODBYE, PIERRE

Out of the pads of Montreal,
Flushed by Levesque and Charles de Gaulle
Came a high-flying cat with a swinging beat,
The Gallic Red Baron of Sussex Street.
There were heroes a-plenty and well known to fame,
Becoming PM was the name of the game
Who in the world could perform such a feat
But the Gallic Red Baron of Sussex Street!

Ten, twenty, thirty, forty ridings or more
Spreading the Tories all over the floor
Who in the world could perform such a feat
But the Gallic Red Baron of Sussex Street!

Parody of Snoopy, 1968

Pierre Trudeau looked better in 1984 than he had in 1968—better physically, that is, if not politically. He had refused to let the killer office of prime minister sap his energies, in part because he had refused to apply all his energies to the job.

He had achieved more personal privacy than any previous prime minister since Mackenzie King, giving media just enough peeks to pique the curiosity of Canadians and the people of the world.

Resurrected in 1980, he had presided over the worst recession since the dirty thirties, and had seen his popularity plunge, and the Liberals in disarray: no Liberal government in any province, only two Liberal MPs in the whole of the West, and the party at 23 per cent in the polls, a figure surpassed on occasion by the NDP.

The conviction gained ground in the Liberal Party that Trudeau must go, but for two years—ever since the patriation of the Constitution—nobody could be found who would bell the cat.

Finally, he belled himself, after long months of indecision in the course of which he very nearly persuaded himself to stay, egged on by his remaining courtiers, Keith Davey, Jim Coutts, and Tom Axworthy. The dread in the party was that Brian Mulroney would beat Trudeau much more decisively than Joe Clark had beaten him in 1979, and it was only slight comfort that the Liberals' slump in the polls reversed itself with Trudeau still in office.

Trudeau finally made his announcement, and the stock market went up 23 points, and within a few weeks the Liberals shot up so shockingly in the Gallup Poll that seasoned observers thought the pollsters had gone crazy.

The message for the Liberals was that they were well rid of him.

But they had to say goodbye in a way that indicated sadness at his leaving, gratitude for a job well done, with none of the negative notes that were the real reason for his going.

The solution hit upon by convention organizers was sheer show biz, and if Trudeau saw through the subterfuge, he didn't say so, though his face may have shown it at the evening's low point, when Paul Anka read, from idiot cards, specially scripted words to his song, "My Way."

There were film clips of the Trudeau highlights, even including a subliminal shot of Margaret with the kids. The audience applauded a quick glimpse of Olympic speedskating hero, Gaetan Boucher, and they cheered the shot of

Trudeau holding his ground against the St. Jean Baptiste Day demonstrators in Montreal, a 1968 election-eve gesture that was worth a hundred thousand votes.

At the start of the evening, before the prime time that the two TV networks had been coerced into conceding, the assembled delegates had to suffer through an interminable hour of chatter by convention co-chairmen Iona Campagnolo and Remi Bujold. She was the leadership candidate who didn't run, and he was the MP for Bonaventure-Iles-de-la-Madeleine, and they prattled away in the manner of ACTRA Award presenters, except there were no awards and nothing to present except a long list of party functionaries.

Finally, it was time to switch on the cameras and bring on the theatricals. On came Myriam, René and Nathalie Simard tapdancing, Nanette Workman. Why were the Liberals doing this at a convention to say goodbye to one prime minister and elect another?

Native Ottawan Rich Little brought some sense to the proceedings with a funny turn featuring his versions of Lester Pearson and John Diefenbaker, with Richard Nixon and Ronald Reagan thrown in for the required American content. He closed with a Trudeau that was not his best, too nasal and not enough shrugging during the sucking in of breath.

Then, horribly, embarrassingly, Ottawa's own Paul Anka giving the crowd exactly what they had paid for— zilch. There he stood, bellowing to his own fine music that Trudeau had made history with national energy, and that "For 16 years you will admit, He stood up tall, against the split."

Good God! There were indoor fireworks that helped a little, but it remained for Trudeau to pick his own farewell evening up off the boards and make it fly.

He pulled it off, without a note, playing on his own emotions and those of the audience, exaggerating, stretching, boasting, prevaricating, and above all, orating and leaving the impression that those who sought to come after him were pygmies in style and mind.

Trudeau's farewell speech will not be long remembered—what Canadian speech ever has been? But it had the old-time merit that you had to be there to get the full flavour, and that the television didn't preserve it, any more than the printed page.

He stretched the truth as far as it would go, and sometimes you could hear it snap—but this was leader's licence, a privilege extended to a man who had put his stamp on so much of recent Canadian history, to the point of claiming that the true, the real, the mature Canada had begun with him.

What arrogance! What presumption! What contempt for the past! Yet arrogance, presumption, and contempt for the past were part of the Trudeau style, and they were among the qualities for which he was most admired, except for those of us in media who felt the sting and responded in kind, without ever leaving a mark on him.

There he stood, I swear, saying that his time in office had been a period of adolescence of our country, a coming of age. Not a word about the previous hundred years of nationhood, making Canada a senior member of the community of nations, and a founder of the Commonwealth concept. Not a word about the two centuries of pre-nationhood, when great events shaped the kind of country Canada would become. Not even the great Franklin D. Roosevelt had claimed to have brought his country to maturity—how could he, when so much that was great, and good, and dreadful had gone before? Not even de Gaulle had claimed to have invented, or re-invented, France.

Trudeau said that his years were "years of turmoil and revolt and search for identity and the slow learning of maturity of our country."

What was the man talking about?

He explained that he was talking about "those values that we see in the Canadian Charter of Rights which for the first time gives all of us an identity rooted in a Constitution that no government can destroy."

Could this be the same Charter of Rights that Trudeau had compromised to get provincial agreement, to the point where he very nearly disowned the document himself? Was this the thing that he had described as deficient, and not the charter he wanted?

Canadians were still pondering, as historians would for decades, whether the flawed Charter was a true human rights document, or a gift to the lawyers who would fatten off its shortcomings.

Yet Trudeau said it was "the people's package," forgetting that his original constitutional "people's package," with its inspirational preamble, was swept away in a welter of federal-provincial discord.

He put it this way, risking that a bolt of lightning would come from above and strike him down: "We said to the people, forget the powers that the premiers want and forget the powers that the federal government wants to keep. Do you want a constitution of your own, do you want us to patriate it, do you want a charter of rights? And the people said yes! And that is how we got it!"

The Supreme Court might demur. Joe Clark might laugh. Roy Romanow and Jean Chrétien, the original Uke and Tuque twosome whose work produced the watered-down compromise, might wonder if they had misheard the prime minister.

No matter, this was his farewell, so he's entitled.

He might even be entitled to this paragraph, coinciding with nobody's recollection of events but his own:

"I remember my caucus and I remember those days in 1980 after the election when we were saying, O.K., we are going to the people. And I said, if we cannot get it from the premiers, we will get it through a referendum. We will ask the people." So far, so good, but from then on it got pretty fuzzy, and the people never did get asked.

Trudeau continued: "Should we get just patriation or should we maybe add some linguistic rights? And the caucus said, hell, no, let us go first class, let us take the whole bag. *On va y aller en Cadillac.* And that is how we got the charter because these men in the caucus and these women said the people want nothing less than first class and they got it."

And still the lightning did not strike him down.

He said he hoped historians would treat him gently, yet he was asking them to draw a line through all that had gone before and give him the main credit for whatever Canada might be, or might become.

He had brought women forward, and Jews, and French Canadians, and Indians, and Eskimos, all sorts of reforms made possible because "I realized that if our cause was right all we had to do to win was to talk over the heads of the premiers, over the heads of the multinationals, over the heads of the superpowers to the people of this land, to the people of Canada."

And when I asked for particulars, I was told that going over the heads of the premiers meant the Constitution, and going over the heads of the multinationals meant Petro Canada, and going over the heads of the superpowers meant the Canadianization of the economy. And going to the people was the election of 1980.

It was vain to protest that the election of 1980 wasn't about any of those things—it was about the perceived deficiencies of the Joe Clark government, and unease about a Tory budget that promised short-term pain for long-term gain, and an 18-cent-a-gallon increase in the price of gasoline, when people still recognized what a gallon was.

Trudeau's farewell speech got, and deserved, a standing ovation from the delegates, with the occasional wet eye in the house, including Trudeau's own.

And when, having finished, he beckoned to his children, saying, *"Allons, enfants de la patrie!"* the three boys trooped up onto the platform and if you weren't crying by then, you were never going to.

Offstage they went, hand in hand, and you could turn to the last page of the glossy magazine got out for the evening, and look at Trudeau paddling off in his canoe, into the sunset.

They gave him a painting, but nobody paid it much attention, amid the oozings of Senator Davey, and Marc Lalonde, and Iona, and Norman Jewison, and last and by all odds least, Paul Anka.

Mercifully, no media people were called on stage for tributes, though we, perhaps, owed him more than any other segment of society, for all he had given us to write about, and writhe about, and for the lamentations he stirred in us to the very end.

Without Pierre Elliott Trudeau, the Grits would never be the same, and neither would we. Dull times loomed, with just one glimmer of hope amid the encroaching gloom. Maybe, just maybe, Jean Chrétien would win, and hilarity would follow.

13

LET THE CANDIDATES SPEAK

Or preferably, you might say, let's not, because they have nothing to say that they haven't been saying for the last two months, which wasn't a hell of a lot.

But convention procedures impose their own disciplines and their own rituals: off with the old, hear from the new, vote and go home.

Candidates' night is supposed to be make-or-break. This was the night in 1968 when Joe Greene won himself an extra couple of dozen votes by making the best speech of his life.

It was the night when Paul Hellyer blew his chance at the Conservative leadership (having missed getting the Liberal leadership ten years earlier) by making a speech attacking Red Tories when the hall was filled with them.

It was the night John Diefenbaker came to pieces and made a bad speech in 1947, falling before George Drew and feeling his political career was at an end.

It was the night Joe Clark sorted himself out from the crowd of back runners and set the stage for his victory the night after. That same night, Brian Mulroney spoke badly and people thought they had seen the last of him.

It was the night for floor demonstrations, except that time constraints had cut these down to a few marchers—no more rocket ships, no more giant scrolls, no more blimps running wild in the rink, à la John Crosbie. And no more nominations—the famous "man who" mouthings—no more seconders. Just the candidates. What you see is what you get.

The draw for the candidates' speeches was ideal from the standpoint of box office—so ideal that there were suspicions of tampering, hotly denied.

Whelan would go first, followed by John Munro, and Mark MacGuigan. Then John Roberts and, building in delegate appeal, Don Johnston. Turner next, and finally Jean Chrétien, counting on the emotional appeal that was the main underpinning of his candidacy. As things turned out, Whelan was the first of the evening's disappointments, and Chrétien was the last.

Whelan's first mistake, if we overlook his error in showing up at all, was to read his speech from a text. His only hope had been to project the earthiness that was his principal contribution to the leadership campaign—that, and his proven expertise in agriculture or, as he termed it, agribusiness.

He started off by attacking Brian Mulroney and Ontario premier William Davis—to him, the Ontario government's failure to train youth for jobs was "disgusting." He would move the federal government in an active way into the field of education, even if it meant invading provincial jurisdiction.

He got in a plug for his theory of collectivization, as reflected in his marketing boards, and he seemed to be saying that, if named leader, he would repeal the law of supply and demand.

He went after the banks, saying he would impose a maximum of 12 per cent on interest rates. Bankers had no feeling, by God, and no concern.

U.S. style Reagonomics amounted to rigor mortis.

The banks had appealed to Trudeau to get the candidates to lay off them in their speeches—"Who the hell do they think they are?"

As for cutting the size of the cabinet, as Turner's

people had said he would do, that would only mean that bureaucrats would run the country.

And he pledged that his deputy prime minister would be a woman, and that she would be put in charge of fisheries, forestry, and agriculture. He closed with the thought that the country had done more for him than he had ever done for the country.

John Munro took up the theme of bank bashing, urging that they give a more generous response to the needs of the people. He was hoarse—the only candidate to have lost his voice in the final round of campaigning—so he had to shout to get the words out. The effect was grotesque as he croaked his praise for the leadership of Trudeau, and called for a healing of divisions between labour and business.

He would end the adversarial approach between the federal government and the provinces, and he would take a gamble on cooperative decision-making—feds and provs, and business, labour and government.

If the Liberals became conservative, the winners would be the Tories. Canadians wanted more, not less, government participation in economic management: they wanted unemployment tackled before the deficit. Unemployment drained the treasury: put people back to work and the deficit would start to melt.

His final appeal was to his natural constituency: labour because of his Hamilton background; and the native peoples because of his work as minister of Indian affairs and northern development.

On came Mark MacGuigan, to proclaim that the Liberal Party had returned from the dead in the last three months, a slap at the Trudeau heritage. He dug the barb in deeper by saying the Trudeau government had been guilty of an outrageous lack of consultation.

Then, in a cut at John Turner, he said proposals to cut the deficit and the size of government were simplistic—reducing unemployment was more important than reducing the federal deficit.

He would "remove the party from the hands of the few and give it back to the Canadian people."

"Give me a hundred women candidates," he went on, "and Mulroney won't stand a chance."

He boasted briefly of his proposed reforms of the criminal code in his role as justice minister, and then he concentrated on his former responsibility, foreign affairs.

He would cut arms spending, work to eliminate the nuclear arms race, give Canada an independent policy in Central and Latin America, and urge the superpowers to cool their dangerous rhetoric. He would de-nuclearize outer space.

He would make Canada a leader of the Third World, the Francophone world, the Commonwealth world. He would keep the Foreign Investment Review Act.

Laurier, King, St. Laurent, and Pearson had been uncharismatic leaders, a comment to which Laurier might well have taken objection. But this was MacGuigan's way of touting his own quiet style—"We can't wait another 100 years for another Pierre Elliott Trudeau."

John Roberts opened his speech with the most direct appeal of the night—"I want very much to lead this party."

He stole a line from Laurier when he said the twenty-first century would be Canada's century, a hundred-year time lag in the ambition expressed by Sir Wilfrid.

Roberts envisioned a Canada that would be a great independent and outward-looking nation, not an appendage of the United States.

He praised "our grand chief, Pierre Trudeau," and he knocked John Turner, saying the bottom line in politics was not balance sheets, but people.

"Do not tip-toe quietly to the right," he said. Do not make the Liberal Party a smudged photocopy of the know-nothing Tories.

He called himself an outsider in a nation built by outsiders, and said he was not the candidate of the party establishment, or the social establishment either.

His biggest cheer, largely from the Chrétien supporters, came when he said "there will be several ballots tomorrow."

It was an eloquent speech but, considering the problem

confronting Roberts' candidacy, utterly inadequate.

Unless Chrétien wins, said one observer, Roberts is cooked.

Up rose Don Johnston, and delegates sat forward in their seats in high expectation. All too soon, they were leaning back, for Johnston could not live up to his press notices, based as they were on his original solutions to the political problems of the day.

Time would not permit a speech on specifics, so he generalized—and Don Johnston generalizing is hardly the stuff of oratory.

He called on delegates to make their choice not on the basis of charm or friendliness (Chrétien) or good looks (Turner). The Tories had found out that beauty was only chin deep—''I'd hate to be Brian Mulroney this evening, he must have smoked half a dozen cigarettes in the last half hour. Make that a dozen.''

Make it zero, in fact. As was well known, Mulroney had given up smoking three weeks before.

The Tories, said Johnston, had slipped from 62 per cent in the polls to 40, proving that image was not enough for the Canadian people. ''They want content.''

''I want to win the leadership of this party more than anything in my entire life, and I want to win the next election even more, for a relevant reason.''

The reason was that he had the road map to the future, and would reject yesterday's solutions. He would do his utmost to bring the nuclear nightmare to an end in a world starving for Canadian sanity. And he would engineer a made-in-Canada interest rate, free of the fiscal misma-nagement south of the border.

Now, amid an ocean of flowing red flags, John Turner.

John Turner might have lost his bid for the Liberal leadership if he had come into the arena that Friday night roaring drunk and fallen off the platform, shouting insults at the assembled delegates.

All he really had to do was voice a few platitudes and keep breathing, but in fact he did a great deal more than that, making what many, including those of us who were his long-time critics, described as the best speech of his life.

His most telling stroke came right at the start, when he paid his respects to Pierre Elliott Trudeau. In some ways, that was the heart of the matter. Turner could not hope for Trudeau's endorsement, and doubtless didn't want it, but for the sake of future peace in the party it was important not to open up the kind of schism that had plagued the Conservatives through so many leaderships.

To pretend friendship or intimacy with Trudeau would be absurd when the ill feelings between the two men had been so visible for so long, underlying Turner's withdrawal from politics and from party affairs in 1975.

To voice unreserved admiration for Trudeau would be hypocritical when so much of Turner's campaign was based on turning a new page, and setting supposed new courses for the much-trumpeted "new Liberalism."

But Turner, with the echoes of the previous night's tribute to Trudeau still reverberating in the hall, paid what he called his personal tribute, calling Trudeau's farewell speech a *tour de force*, which it certainly was.

He said it would not be easy for any of the candidates to succeed Trudeau, which it certainly would not.

And he called Trudeau the most remarkable Canadian of our generation, which could mean many things depending on the definition of remarkable. Certainly, no one in media would quarrel with that description of Trudeau, nor would we have cavilled had Turner called Trudeau the most remarkable prime minister Canada had ever had.

Then Turner said of Trudeau that "no Canadian deserves more credit than the prime minister," long pause, "in his search for peace."

Having thus settled accounts with his old leader and tormentor, Turner was at his ease and started saying things that, by implication, indicated how harmful Trudeau's leadership really had been.

"I can offer," he said, "a leadership that will bring us back to a mood of confidence. We will be a united party, a party renewed, a truly national party again. . . . There is a sense of urgency abroad in our land. . . . Give me your vote and we will rebuild the Liberal Party into a new coalition, and we will win the next general election.''

Right on, cheered his growing mass of delegate supporters.

Turner didn't fill in many of the details, and he didn't repeat his pledge, early in the campaign, to cut the federal deficit by half in the next five years—the old right-wing stuff that many thought, and still think, represented the true John Turner.

Instead, he said that nothing he did would be undertaken at the expense of the underprivileged. Universality of social programs would stay, and no programs would be dismantled.

He would support affirmative action, equality for women in the workforce. That would be part of a new era of issues that he would tackle.

"I will support the family farm," said the man in the three-piece suit who looked and sounded as though he had never seen a farm, much less worked one. "I will encourage young people to remain on the land."

Then he turned to his international experience, and said he would get out and sell Canadian products abroad.

He would make the West a true partner in Confederation—incredibly, he was the only candidate to address himself specifically to Western concerns.

He boasted that throughout the campaign he had not fought Liberals, but had aimed his criticism at Conservatives.

The man who had himself been called a small-c conservative dubbed Brian Mulroney a "let's pretend Liberal," noting that Mulroney had agreed with Liberal policies on medicare, women's rights, and language.

Conveniently overlooking the policies the Liberals had kidnapped from the Conservatives, he said "Canadians won't buy a let's pretend Liberal, they will choose a real Liberal every time."

Was Turner, though, a "real" Liberal?

His speech left the question hanging, but for the moment it didn't matter, though it might matter a great deal in times to come, and delegates studying the Turner record in recent years had only Bay Street to go by.

They gave him a standing ovation, and then it was Jean Chrétien's turn.

For John Turner, this may or may not have been the speech of his life.

For Jean Chrétien, it almost certainly was. If speeches could sway undecided delegates, then he had to surpass the high expectations that were held for him, the reports from his campaign speeches having been so glowing.

He knew there was still a gap between his delegate support and Turner's. He didn't know how wide it was, but he hoped it was less than 300, because anything more than that would be hard to close on a second or third ballot, if indeed it could be closed at all.

He knew that as the only French-speaking candidate he had to draw a nice balance between English and French in his speech.

And he knew he had to speak from his heart, yet not be so emotional that the speech would be criticized for lack of substance. He had to sound like a man who could be prime minister.

Knowing all these things, he made the fatal mistake of choosing to speak from a prepared text, having resolved right up to late afternoon not to do so.

Thus imprisoned, Chrétien was strapped in from the start, and could not fly as he had throughout the campaign, tossing off quips amid the heartfelt things he said about Canada, and Canadians, and his own record of long and distinguished service to party and country.

His opening remarks were addressed to Brian Mulroney, who had been aching for some mention and must have rejoiced to have his name going out from the Liberal convention, in prime time, first from Turner's lips, and now from Chrétien's.

"Brian, Brian," Chrétien read from his notes, "do not adjust your TV set. What you see is what you are going to get.'' And he counselled Mulroney to spend as much as he liked making Stornaway, the opposition residence, comfortable, because the Tory leader would be there for a long, long time.

"I want to lead the Liberal Party," said Chrétien. "I am part of the Liberal record and I am proud of it." He had no apology to make for the record of Trudeau, whose legacy was for all. Chrétien had served with pride for sixteen years, through good years and bad.

Then he went into one of those litanies that evoke audience responses, but the script threw his timing off.

Should we distance ourselves from the party's heritage?

No! chanted the audience, but Chrétien didn't wait for it, mouthing the scripted words, "not this Liberal."

He kept asking the rhetorical questions and the audience kept giving the right answers, and he kept saying "not this Liberal."

"I will not move this great party to the right," he said, "I will move it forward."

Then, another litany, handled more stiffly than the one before.

Equality? "I will be satisfied with nothing less."

Peace? "I will be satisfied with nothing less."

A strong economy? The audience tried to shout in a chorused "yes," but Chrétien overrode with "I will be satisfied with nothing less."

He went after Turner—"We are not choosing a chief executive officer, we are choosing a political leader."

Some delegates were struggling to vote with their hearts, and they should yield to the impulse—"We built the country because we had the heart."

Then he voiced a sentiment with which many Conservatives, especially Quebec Conservatives, had come to agree, watching Chrétien campaign.

"Can I beat Brian Mulroney? Yes, I can. But the real question is whether we can beat the Tories and maintain our principles.

"You must decide. You must decide. I want to be that leader and I need your help.

"Vive le Canada!"

Prolonged cheers, in the midst of which everybody in our broadcast booth agreed that if the speech of his life was needed to save Chrétien's candidacy, he had fallen short. He had made a better speech than that at almost every stop in the campaign, and at every policy session, and he had often spoken better than that in the House of Commons, that graveyard of orators.

If I could have got my hands on whoever persuaded Chrétien to read from a text, I would have throttled him—but later I learned that the decision was Chrétien's own, in the interest of statesmanship.

And statesmen, I mused, are sometimes described as politicians who are out of work.

The full magnitude of what they were being called upon to do did not seem to hit the delegates until voting day, Saturday, when they went to the coolness of the Ottawa Civic Centre to cast their ballots.

The temperature was a blessing, thanks be to God, who showed again that She might indeed be a Grit. This convention was spared the sweltering heat that had broiled Conservative delegates a year ago when they gathered for their lesser rite of either confirming the existing opposition leader, Joe Clark, or electing a new one, either Brian Mulroney or John Crosbie.

The idea of thirty-five hundred men and women deciding who would lead the opposition in Parliament did not seem too outrageous, even though the main contender to Clark had never sat in Parliament in his life, and had never run for elected office of any kind.

But the idea of so few people electing a man who would govern in the name of all Canadians seemed awesome to some, and outrageous to others. In twos and threes they had come from selected villages, towns, and cities across the land, and most places had sent no delegates at all. One-quarter of the delegates were young people, and over half were women. The under-represented segment of society, in social terms, was the segment that would have the most political clout by the turn of the century, the seniors.

Supporters of other political parties would have no vote

in this election for prime minister. And many of those who would be voting were not long-time Liberals—their credentials varied depending on what part of the country they came from.

The prime minister these delegates selected would replace a man who had been confirmed as head of government by vote of the entire Canadian electorate, not once but four times. His name was firmly imprinted on what would be known in Canadian political history as the Trudeau era.

It was the dregs of Trudeau's final mandate, now well into its fifth year, that would be handed to the new prime minister. Not much of a prize, people said, but still it would carry with it as many of the peaks and perks of power as would be gained in a landslide election victory.

Indeed, if we are to believe that the powers of the prime minister's office have come to surpass those of Parliament itself, this convention process would influence national affairs more than a general election.

Says Dalton Camp: "Now that the parties don't have any influence left in the policy area, the only power left to a party is to elect a leader. And the only power left to the constituency organizations is to say who gets nominated. If you take that away, everyone becomes a eunuch."

Yet the riding associations sent less than 65 per cent of the Liberal delegates, and nearly half of those were elected by quota to make up for the fact that the Liberals had no member of parliament or legislatures west of Winnipeg. Thirty five per cent of the convention delegates were members of parliament, ex-officio functionaries, and "others." Assuming that each riding assembled 500 people to choose convention delegates (a large assumption), you could come up with a figure of 140,000 Canadians who were involved in the convention process, about half of one percent of the population.

As Ian Brown pointed out in the Toronto *Globe and Mail*, primary elections in the United States involve 13 per cent of American voters, a much broader base of public participation. Even in the shock of the assassination or natural death of a president, the U.S. system hands the succession to a vice-president who has been part of the winning ticket in the previous election. It is hard to imagine a Wall Street lawyer being handed the U.S. presidency by vote of a single political party, though Richard Nixon used a Wall Street sabbatical as preparation for his 1968 come-back. In coming back, he had first to pass muster with the Republican Party in convention assembled, and then with the electorate.

To elect Canada's new prime minister, the Liberal apparatus recommended that nobody under the age of fourteen should have a voice in choosing convention dele-gates. In most provinces, a seventy-two-hour deadline was imposed on the admission of new party members, three days being deemed long enough to make a person a Grit. A lot of three-day Liberals emerged, checked somewhat by a requirement that parachuters from outside a riding must have held membership cards for a minimum of six months.

Regulations varied among the 282 riding associations, each of which sent seven voting delegates and seven alternatives to the convention, plus the riding association president and the sitting MP, or the candidate defeated in the last election or the nominee for the coming one.

Once the delegates were chosen, the pollsters went to work on them, claiming more scientific results than they could get in polls sampling the entire population.

And because of computers, one organizer cracked that never have so many known so much about so few—every candidate had print outs on every delegate's first choice preference, second choice, and third choice, the "anybody but" choice. The standings were reviewed every morning, and when the batteries of computers weren't being used to keep score, they were put to work churning out personal-ized letters to delegates, leading one recipient to joke that "people try to sell me eternal light bulbs that way."

The human factor still counted, as much as it had in the days of the smoke-filled rooms, and manipulators like Turner's Bill Lee still drew gasps of admiration, while the gurus of the past paraded before the television cameras with reflections on past glories and present probabilities.

Without facing the voters at all, the new prime minister would take over the most powerful office in the land, and one of the most powerful in the western world.

The setting of policy lines would be his, as well as the appointment and firing of cabinet ministers, the global attitudes of the Canadian government, the handling of the biggest payroll and the biggest deficit in Canadian history, the setting of an election date, and such small matters as moving into the prime ministerial premises at 24 Sussex Drive and Harrington Lake. The swimming pool, the $250,000 Cadillac, and all the myriad pieces of puffery that go with being prime minister, all would be bestowed by these thirty-five hundred people, the great majority of whom came into the arena with their minds made up.

Indeed, a majority had come to Ottawa already decided, influenced by a variety of factors the most decisive of which were the public opinion polls. If John Turner's candidacy had been inspired and sustained by one major factor, it was those polls and the media coverage that stemmed from and was shaped by them.

It was from the polls that the impression of Turner emerged as the man who could win an election. If Turner won, he would be the first prime minister in history to be selected, if not elected, by public opinion poll, with most of his supporters saying they really didn't care for him very much but they wanted a winner.

Polls had played an important part in the Conservative convention the year before, but that was for opposition leader and not prime minister, so the job was purely partisan and not a fraction as important to the entire population. Guided by the polls, the Tories had rejected a leader with a sadly weak chin, and chosen a man with a hilariously strong one.

And polls had been a factor in 1968, when Trudeau was chosen, but in his case they reflected a wave of emotion that turned into a mania, inspired by one of the most unusual men ever to offer himself for office anywhere in the world.

This time, the polls had been operating in cold blood, reflecting support for a Bay Street tycoon who generated little emotion, but a great deal of respect. And in the three days of the leadership convention you could sense the mood—the Turner parties were reserved affairs, in contrast to the wild enthusiasm of the Chrétien camp. By voting day, poll results were flying around like confetti. A Martin Goldfarb poll, commissioned by millionaire developer Robert Campeau, showed Turner would lose to Mulroney, but that Chrétien might win. The Turner camp cried foul—Campeau is a long-time pal of Chrétien (and of Trudeau), and he comes from Sudbury you see, and so does millionaire Paul Demarais, and Chrétien's daughter is married to Demarais' son, you see. Besides which, John Rae, Chrétien's campaign manager, works for Desmarais, you know.

The Turner camp came whistling back with a poll of their own, conducted by Winnipeg pollster Angus Reid, a protégé of Lloyd Axworthy. His figures showed that Turner could beat the Conservatives and Chrétien could not.

In a contest so heavily influenced by polls, it was not unfitting that the pollsters themselves should be in the thick of the battle and that, in the subsequent debacle, Martin Goldfarb would be among the casualties. It was a sign of the times. Up to now, when leaderships changed, it was advertising agencies that got dumped. They still do, but now they have been joined by a more important political breed, the pollsters.

Even journalists, once classed as an important if not a vital ingredient in politics (the Fourth Estate, remember?) found their output being shaped and displaced by poll results—polls purchased by newspapers and networks, or commissioned by them and given a featured place in campaign coverage, with editors clamouring for more.

On voting day, the Liberal hall was much more orderly than it had been with the Tories the year before. Even the Liberal campaign posters were hung neatly in rows, and there had been no fistfights among the pasters and staplers, nor did anybody put posters over the air conditioning vents as those crazy Tories had.

The hall was full of people who were concerned about their asses, which tends to make them look preoccupied, the normal facial expression in a capital where "cover your ass" is a watchword.

The men and women packed tightly around the winner would have much to gain, which is why so many Liberal MPs and cabinet ministers were packed around John Turner.

Rich prizes might await those around Jean Chrétien, but it was a long shot, which was why Chrétien was able to say that he would arrive at 24 Sussex with very little baggage.

There were some whose days were numbered, though the only one admitting the fact openly was Pierre Trudeau who, on this final day of his leadership, was realizing the full impact of the things he would lose, not the least of which was the attention of press and public, in which he had revelled so long while pretending not to.

Filled as he was with his lasting sense of the inadequacies of other men, he must have brooded about how inferior Turner was to himself, a view that he had made clear through the years.

And he must have lamented Chrétien's inadequacies, as he would have scorned Chrétien had they met as kids: Chrétien the seventeenth of nineteen kids born in a tarpaper shack in Shawinigan; Trudeau the spoiled millionaire brat in Montreal. Chrétien grew up punching other kids in the nose. Trudeau punished his foes by denying them rides in his father's chauffeur-driven limousine. Trudeau's father, Charlie, would have had more in common with Chrétien than with his own son, and Trudeau himself shared the reservations of the Quebec elite about Chrétien's candidacy, but he kept his silence, secure in the knowledge that Turner had paid him public respect the night before.

John Turner entered the hall for the voting with the sublime inner confidence of a man who knows he is going to win, and is already shaping his moves for the time when power is his.

Jean Chrétien carried with him the delicious contemplation that he might win, he just might, but he kept saying it would be hard.

In a calloused age and a calloused political party, it was possible to be moved by the Chrétien supporters, who so obviously believed in their man and felt themselves involved in a crusade of people versus the machine. You got the feeling there were people who would die for Chrétien, and the remarkable thing was that the numbers included so many more English-speakers than French-speakers.

From the Chrétien seats, there were waves of cheers, with the candidate himself leading the roars. And they cheered the other candidates, too, all but Turner. The better the other candidates did in the first ballot, the better Chrétien's chances—or so went the reasoning.

In his own mind, Mark MacGuigan had already accepted defeat and had made his decision to go to the winner, Turner, on the second ballot. His thinking was heavily influenced by the defection of his prime supporter, Edmonton Mayor Laurence Decore, who obviously felt he had paid whatever personal debt he owed to MacGuigan and knew that if his career as a Liberal were to flower, it would do so in Turner's garden. MacGuigan's decision was as honourable as anything can be when political tradeoffs are flying, but it would earn him the undying hatred of the Chrétien supporters, who would boo him before the day was out.

Don Johnston had cast himself in the losing Turner role from the 1968 convention—sure that he would be Number Three, knowing that Number Three was nowhere, but convinced he had done himself nothing but good during the campaign. He would hang in to the end, and take his own bright career chances with the winner; as Turner had in 1968 with Trudeau, enduring short term pain for eventual long-term gain.

John Roberts clung to his dwindling hopes of finishing Number Three on the first ballot, but had already made up his mind to go to Chrétien on the second.

John Munro was thinking the same, and so was Eugene Whelan.

All of them had to approach the first vote looking and sounding like winners—the first great cruelty of leadership conventions, the second being the requirement to look brave in losing, pretending admiration for the winner.

The clock moved with agonizing slowness. For all the slick computers of the candidates, the Liberals were still using manual ballots and counting them by hand, the only rapid aspect being the instant printing of the ballots themselves—on yellow paper for the first vote, green paper for the second.

There may have been method in the primitive vote-counting procedure, since the balloting opened at 2 p.m. on the Saturday afternoon, and the objective was to carry things through into TV prime time in the evening, it being reckoned that every minute on the networks was worth $2,000 in publicity—and publicity was the stuff of an upward climb in the polls, which in turn could mean election victory.

As the polls opened, reporters poked microphones in the faces of all the candidates.

"It has been a very civilized fight," said Jean Chrétien.

"No deals at all," said Johnston. When he left abruptly to go to the bathroom, he said, "I'm off to make a deal."

John Turner's contribution was to say, "One never knows. We're going to win it sooner or later." And that was the truest thing anybody said during this longest of long campaign days and nights.

No sooner had the polls been declared open under the hockey rink bleachers than Allan MacEachen created a sensation by showing up in the Turner box.

The surprise was not so much his decision to support Turner, though an old reformer like MacEachen might have felt happier in Chrétien's company, and he had no reason to remember with gratitude or admiration the manner of Turner's quitting the Trudeau team in 1975.

No, the surprise was in MacEachen's timing, designed for maximum psychological effect on delegates, and optimum negative impact on the Chrétien forces. MacEachen let it be known that he had made up his mind to support

Turner weeks ago, though he said everything had fallen into place on Friday night with Turner's speech—a presumed reference to Turner's praise of Trudeau.

"Turner can lead us to victory; he's a real Liberal; I will be his loyal servant."

Minutes later, I sat in the same broadcast booth with MacEachen and Tory John Crosbie, and Crosbie congratulated MacEachen on becoming Turner's new "boozum boody." Crosbie called MacEachen "the first Cassius" and predicted Finance Minister Marc Lalonde would be the second. Then he said: "This is the final shaft up poor Chrétien's fundament. That means arse."

Maybe MacEachen wasn't needed by Turner, and perhaps his action was not such a blow to Chrétien as it appeared, since Chrétien had known it was coming. What hurt more was Chrétien's knowledge that if Turner didn't make it on the first or second ballot, Marc Lalonde would declare for Turner, meaning that all his senior Quebec colleagues were against him.

For three hours, the talking heads of television kept switching around and discussing what was happening, which was that votes were cast and counted and the results were being stalled, and what wasn't, which was a deal to stop John Turner.

The excitement, apart from MacEachen (who got on all the shows as soon as he had joined, and left, Turner's side) was Mayor Laurence Decore of Edmonton, who quit Mac-Guigan before the ballots were counted. MacGuigan sagged at the sight of Decore going over to Turner, and said he thought they were supposed to stick together until the first vote was announced.

As soon as it was, MacGuigan was over at Turner's side, before you could say "every man for himself." MacGuigan has a kind of a fawning smile that had not stood him in good stead during the campaign, when he tried to keep his dignity as a former foreign affairs minister and a distinguished minister of justice. Turner's smile is not known for its lasting warmth and he didn't exactly melt at MacGuigan's arrival, though the man had collected 135 votes on the first ballot, ten more than Turner would need on ballot number two to win.

Whelan finished last, with 84, very nearly overtaking Munro, with 93. MacGuigan's 135 put him fifth, Roberts was fourth with 185, Johnston third with 278, Chrétien second at 1,067, and Turner tops with 1,593.

The number needed to win was 1,718, so Turner had failed to make it on the first ballot. Pre-convention wisdom was that things should open up if Turner could be stopped at the start, so there was a mixed buzz of hope and despair in the Chrétien camp. Altogether, there had been 1,909 votes for candidates other than Turner—but could they be described as anti-Turner votes?

Whelan walked to Chrétien, having to fight his way through the crowd on the convention floor. Nobody could tell how many of his delegates followed him.

Then came Munro to the Chrétien bleachers, and finally, John Roberts, carrying what one writer described as the burden of his grief. Again, you couldn't tell how many of their followers followed them—but Munro's campaign director, Isabel Finnerty, and his chief media man, Hugh Rushford, went to Turner.

Would Johnston move? His 278 votes were serious, so Chrétien went to him and they had a long palaver, while the Chrétien cheering section shouted "Johnston" and "D.J." and the Roberts' jazz band from the University of Saskatoon switched to Chrétien lyrics for their version of Glen Miller's "Pennsylvania 6-5000."

Johnston had been hitting foam tennis balls over into the Chrétien section, and Chrétien had autographed one of them and thrown it back, but all Johnston gave him for his pains this time was a slap on the back. Johnston said later he didn't move to Chrétien because it was clear Turner was going to win, and he didn't want to create the impression of a gang-up against Turner.

Chrétien said he would never quit. "It's not mission impossible, but it's a tough situation. And I love tough situations."

His people kept working the floor during the long delay before the taking of the second ballot, and Chrétien kept shouting "let's go" until he was hoarse. Prime TV rolled around, and suddenly Turner had a bigger police guard than before, bigger than anybody else, and at 8:31 Iona Campagnolo and René Bujold announced that they were going for the results, returning immediately to the podium.

Chrétien, 1,368, a gain of 301 from his first ballot total.

There was a momentary cheer from the Chrétien supporters, before they realized how far short their man had fallen. They knew in a moment—Turner, 1,862. And lost in the bedlam, Johnston at 192.

Not a coronation—Chrétien had done his job by creating at least the illusion of a contest. He had done it so well that in the subsequent hubbub of the Turner victory, Campagnolo drew cheers when she said that Chrétien had finished second in the votes, "but first in our hearts." These were strange words for Turner to hear moments after securing the leadership and the prime ministership that goes with it, but he didn't quibble. In his victory speech, he said Chrétien was the most popular member of the party, adding that he recognized his strength and wanted it to continue.

It had taken Turner ten minutes to get to the platform, keeping all the defeated candidates waiting, along with Pierre Trudeau, who stood at the far left of the stage, his face inscrutable, his thoughts perhaps going back to the night sixteen years ago when the triumph was his, and he had clutched that rose in his teeth.

People who run for public office do so for a variety of grand or petty motives, and in four decades of observing politics I am still puzzled about why candidates seek the punishment of victory or defeat.

But I do know that anyone who runs for the top office of prime minister had better have a high motive for doing so. And the prime reason for running must be a belief that of all the available candidates, you are the one most suited to the job.

John Turner had believed that for twenty years and longer.

Jean Chrétien had come to believe it in the last dozen years, and had built a record of political achievement to back his claim.

Donald Macdonald, who had a chance at the Liberal leadership snatched away from him in 1979, when Trudeau changed his mind about retiring, said he felt relieved. And when somebody expressed disbelief, he likened the job to Sisyphus rolling a stone uphill with his nose. "You feel grateful when somebody takes the stone away," he said.

Macdonald's view is not that of your average leadership candidate, confirming what he once said about himself, that he lacked the royal jelly.

Turner was born with it and Chrétien developed it, as did Brian Mulroney. Joe Clark didn't have enough of it, and Pierre Trudeau didn't give it a thought. As to the John Munros, Eugene Whelans, John Roberts and Mark Mac-Guigans of politics, they create fantasies about themselves and are sustained to the moment of truth, and then they have a rationale for what happens that saves their faces, at least with themselves. There are always some of them in any leadership contest, and parents who encourage their children to go into politics should use these people as horror stories.

They should look, too, at Chrétien after Turner's victory was announced, and see him trying to project an image of grace when all about him were weeping, as Tories had wept around Joe Clark a year earlier.

The photographs of Chrétien's face in defeat are as extraordinary as the shots of him in exultation during the campaign. His incredible, malleable features can twist into a series of caricatures that conceal whether he is happy or sad.

Most delegates were too preoccupied with victory or defeat to pay attention to the closing speeches at the convention: Chrétien's concession, and Turner's victory speech. But both speeches went beyond the pro forma mouthings usual on such occasions, and Chrétien's in particular was full of nuances, provoked as he was by expressions of affection from all sides of the hall, tempered by the message that delegates didn't think he was up to the top job.

Chrétien took the microphone, and he hogged it. He seemed to be paying tribute to Turner without really doing so, apart from his motion that the Turner victory be made unanimous. Obviously, he would rather have moved that it be reversed and that the delegates give him their votes along with their hearts. What he said to Turner was this:

"I offer him my friendship, my best wishes, and I assure him a united Liberal party. He can be sure that, when it comes time for the next election, the Liberal principles will be the philosophy that leads us into the next election."

What the hell was that supposed to mean?

Turner didn't bother to look beneath the surface of Chrétien's words, though he might have occasion to in the days and weeks ahead.

Turner's own "impromptu" victory speech, pre-scripted and bound in leather, had been handed over the apron of the stage by an aide, and Geills Turner had to dash forward to take delivery of it and return it to her husband.

Thus equipped, Turner approached the rostrum and gave a speech that was long on wind and short on content—the very model of your average speech from the throne, which indeed it may well have been.

He pledged to lead a new coalition of Canadians forging a new brand of Liberalism. That kind of promise had served him well through the campaign, and it had carried the convention, and it would form the basis for an election campaign. Within hours, billboards were going up across the country bearing Turner's portrait and the new Grit slogan, "Today we celebrate our future."

If Turner babbled on and on, so did Chrétien, talking about Liberal principles. Perhaps he did it to keep himself from crying, but he kept talking about Liberal principles to the point where talk-weary reporters turned away to the task of reporting the prime news of Turner's victory, and unleashing the flood of packaged biographies and sidebars on the winner. Nobody had bothered to put much stuff about Chrétien into the bank, just as the Liberals had prepared no billboards against the eventuality of a Chrétien win.

But Turner wasn't finished—into the crowded Civic Centre newsroom came the announcement of a Turner press conference, to take place immediately.

Turner made it easy for the networks by holding the press conference from the main arena stage, and he took questions as long as reporters could think of them. The TV networks cut away as soon as their reporters had asked their on-camera questions, Craig Oliver of CTV acting as though he owned Turner, perhaps because of the wilderness canoe connection. Turner held forth.

He said Chrétien could have a cabinet job if he wanted one.

He said reporters wouldn't expect him to give them the election date, though obviously they did.

The shape of his new cabinet would take a number of days to determine. He would let reporters know who was in it when they were sworn in.

He wanted candidates of quality in the West.

He would give a new look to Canadian foreign policy, setting up better relations with the United States. He would create jobs.

By the time work was finished, it was almost midnight, and time to go to the Liberal victory party, where members of what had been the John Roberts jazz band were standing hip deep in a fountain pool, still playing at the top of their lungs.

"There could be only one winner," Jean Chrétien had said, "and I'm not the one." Next day, he had nothing to say to reporters, and he said it in French: "*Pas de commentaires.*"

He spent much of the day visiting the dozens of volunteers who had worked for him, touring the hotels, thanking everybody including the cab drivers for whom he had given a lunch at the start of the convention. People said how nice it was that having elected Turner, the party would be getting Chrétien too, just as the Turner campaigners had promised. Chrétien swore, in French.

14

MULRONEY

So it would be "Bones" Mulroney versus "Chick" Turner in a fight to the finish.

Bones was the name hung on Mulroney by his classmates at St. Francis Xavier University in Antigonish, when the boy from Baie Comeau put down his Nova Scotia roots.

And Chick was Turner's own nickname for himself during his time at the University of British Columbia, where he lived like a rich kid while insisting he wasn't.

Mulroney's background was blue-collar, while Turner's was more Top Hat. Mulroney supported his mother and the family after his electrician father died, while Turner was supported by his widowed mother until the legal fees started to come in.

Turner used a political career as a springboard to fortune in the corporate world. Mulroney used a career in the corporate world as a springboard to political leadership.

Mulroney had to wrestle leadership of the Conservative Party from the incumbent, Joe Clark. Turner had leadership of the Liberal Party thrust upon him by the voluntary, if belated, retirement of Pierre Trudeau. And if there was bad blood between Mulroney and Clark, there was even deeper hostility between Trudeau and Turner. Had it not been for Mulroney's accession to the Tory leadership, Trudeau might have felt impelled to stay for another election. So we can say with some truth that the man who was the root cause of the whole Liberal leadership imbroglio was Mulroney, and that he caused the Liberals to pick John Turner over Jean Chrétien, because Turner's vibes were like Mulroney's, only stronger and more reassuring to investors.

And Mulroney was the one who drove the Liberals to their all-time low in the public opinion polls, threatening the New Democrats with extinction in the process.

These things happened at a time when the Liberals were able to extend their mandate to its limit, avoiding an election showdown and in the process inventing the theory that the Canadian tradition is for majority governments to hold office for a full five years, instead of four.

Had there been an election in 1983, Mulroney and the Progressive Conservatives would have had a victory rivalling that of John Diefenbaker in 1958, though not even Mulroney in his wildest moments could have hoped to match Diefenbaker's 50 Tory seats in Quebec.

But there was no election, and Trudeau used the intervening borrowed time to stage his peace initiative, and finally, reluctantly, to declare he was ready to lay down his leadership, even if it meant opening the way for the despised John Turner.

And it was in that same timespan that some of the magic wore off Mulroney, putting aside any chance that there might have been an outbreak of "Mulroomania" to match the Trudeaumania of 1968.

There were several reasons for Mulroney's decline in popularity, not the least of which was that it is difficult to hold centre stage when you are leader of the opposition, and when the election timing is in other hands. Trudeau couldn't have whipped up his 1968 mania from the opposition benches—it's easier when you are in power, or have it handed to you, as happened to Trudeau and now to Turner.

Another reason was that Trudeau's own popularity started to climb back up because of his peace initiative, in which he used his global stature, such as it was, in the cause of peace and nuclear de-escalation. Here again, a new opposition leader could not contend with the impact of a man who, because of tenure, had become the senior statesman of the western world, a world that had scarcely heard of Mulroney.

And the final reason was Mulroney's own decision, as leader of the opposition, to oppose government policies rather than proposing policies of his own. In this, he was following the tradition of opposition leaders in all parliamentary democracies, a tradition rigidly observed by the Liberal Party of Canada on the few occasions in which it was out of power.

The Grits in opposition, against John Diefenbaker and Joe Clark (or R.B. Bennett, if you want to go back that far), had only one idea, and that was to throw the rascals out. To this end, they resorted to every tactic of obstruction and destruction they could lay their hands on. Their plotters were men like Jack Pickersgill and Allan MacEachen, whose fame (and eventual fortune) rested on getting the Liberals back into power as quickly as possible, by hook or by crook.

Never, certainly, by proposing alternate policies to those of the Conservative governments.

The lesson was that oppositions exist to oppose, and it was driven home by the only opposition leader ever to propose comprehensive policies, Robert Stanfield. In the election of 1974, he took the suicidal course of proposing wage-and-price controls to cure the economic ills of the time, and both the Liberals and New Democrats ran their entire campaigns against Stanfield, who became known as the greatest prime minister who never was.

The Liberals added insult to injury by adopting Stanfield's policy a year later, but that was small satisfaction to the man who left politics without ever accomplishing the great things of which he was capable, though he wound up as the only politician in the country without an enemy.

So Mulroney elected to play the opposition role in the traditional way, staying on the attack as much as possible and saving his major policy pronouncements for election time, while at the same time indicating his natural conservative lean and his pre-disposition for closer and more cordial relations with the United States.

He took the progressive line on medicare and on French language rights in Manitoba, avoiding Liberal attempts to sandbag him on both issues, but offending provincial Tories and some members of his own federal caucus in the process.

He supported continued universality of social programs in the face of doubts voiced by, among others, his Newfoundland honcho John Crosbie.

He backed equal rights for women, though with the same tentative stance of Turner on the issue, and without the wholehearted commitment of Joe Clark.

At the same time, he brought Clark and his entire entourage onside by naming them to important posts in the shadow cabinet and the party apparatus, to the point of throwing confusion into the ranks of those who had supported him against Clark for the leadership.

This perhaps was his greatest achievement, and observers said that any man who could bring the Conservative Party together must be eminently qualified for the simpler job of governing a fractious Canada.

But Mulroney's caution on policy declarations took its toll in terms of public opinion. Since he lacked a political track record prior to becoming Tory leader, voters and critics had nothing to measure him by, and so the impression gained ground that he not only had nothing old to offer, he had nothing new, either. Those around Mulroney denied it hotly, but more and more, as I moved about the country, I heard people talking about Mulroney, in the Nova Scotian phrase, being ''all swank and no knickers.''

The public opinion polls showed the change of mood almost from the moment of Pierre Trudeau's retirement announcement. There was a momentary blip upward in the Gallup for the Tories, followed by a 14-point surge that lifted the Liberals from the depths into a 6-point lead.

There had never been so dramatic a shift in a public

opinion poll on politics, and there was a general disposition to imagine that the Gallup had erred. But a month later the figures showed up again, and the Liberals became believers, and the Tories became doubters, their spirits sustained only by Mulroney's coolness in the face of bad news.

It was all a bulge caused by the Liberal leadership campaign, he said, and when we get into an election campaign it will all come right again. Yet there were signs that his own popularity surge in Quebec had subsided, and Quebec Tories needed a strong pull from Mulroney to break their jinx in that province. At 28 per cent in the polls, the Conservatives were still higher than they had been in years in Quebec, but it was a slip from 36 per cent in February—and even 36 per cent was not enough to guarantee the winning of Quebec seats.

And while the two parties were virtually even in Ontario, there were signs of a Liberal re-awakening in the West. Again, perhaps not enough to win seats, but at least enough to prevent a Tory sweep of the West, enabling the New Democrats to hold at least some of their western seats, all of which had been in jeopardy at the turn of the year.

So Mulroney, having played a key role in forcing the retirement of Trudeau, was now the central figure in the coming election—if he could not cut the mustard in Quebec, and if he could not hold the West, there seemed a real prospect that the Liberals under John Turner would retain power.

Mulroney's prospects were at least as good as Turner's—but six months previously, he had had the Trudeau-led Liberals on the ropes.

He put the time of the Liberal leadership campaign to good use, spending forty-six days on the road, most of them in the company of his biggest asset, his wife, Mila. Up and down the land they went, most of the visits being to out-of-the-way places that would have to be flown over in an election campaign. Everywhere Mulroney went, the local media impact was strong, and he got to press the flesh of a lot of Canadians who had never seen a national party leader, and who would certainly not get to see John Turner before or during an election.

Turner was concentrating on Liberal convention delegates, while Mulroney was moving among the people at large. And at the height of the Liberal leadership excitement, he made news by reaching an energy pact with Newfoundland Premier Brian Peckford, ensuring that if a Conservative government came to power in Ottawa, Newfoundland would be given the same rights to offshore oil resources that Alberta enjoys in oilfields within her borders.

And Mulroney's visit to Washington in the days after the Liberal convention was a triumph of sorts, underlying Mulroney's own determination to warm up relations between the two countries, and a chance to exchange blarney with that other chip off the old stone, Ronald Reagan.

Patently, the Conservatives had a more appealing leader in Mulroney than they had previously with Clark—just as Clark, in turn, had lifted the party to heights beyond Robert Stanfield's reach. Clark had gained stature by his grace under pressure during the long questioning of his leadership, ending with his being unseated by Mulroney. Now, Clark seemed prepared to put his stature at Mulroney's disposal, at least for one all-out election campaign.

Mulroney would need more than that. Like Turner, he would need new faces, and hopefully some "name" candidates who would beef up his claim that he was the master administrator, and that his great strength was with people. Obviously, he was a good delegater, but equally obviously, there had to be strong people to whom he could delegate power. John Crosbie was there, and Michael Wilson, and Sinclair Stevens. The Tory premiers were supportive, as they never had been of Clark—though Mulroney, if he came to power, might wish that somebody would save him from his friends. He promised to be conciliatory in federal-provincial dealings, and in this, as in many other areas, John Turner promptly lifted the Mulroney line and made it his own.

This was a final reason for Mulroney's caution in outlining policy: the Liberals were as quick to pick up Conservative ideas as they once were at picking the policy bones of the NDP and its predecessor, the CCF.

Mulroney stayed coy about where he would run in a general election, the expectation being that he would pick a riding in Quebec. He taunted Turner to run in British Columbia, and Turner obliged by saying he would. But Mulroney held off picking the Quebec riding of his choice, knowing that the instant he identified the place, the Liberals would treat it as a bottomless pit of federal patronage and favours. Whatever riding Mulroney would pick was bound to have a Liberal incumbent, Pierre Trudeau's stranglehold on his native province having been so complete.

The biggest obstacle in Mulroney's way was the impression that the Liberal Party had somehow been reborn, despite the fact that the leadership change took place with the 1980 mandate almost exhausted. Media, which had turned critical of Turner after the initial adulation, reverted to an attitude of respectful attention to his pronouncements and his long-range plans for government re-organization, even though these could be little more than election pronouncements.

And Mulroney had to reckon with the widespread impression that the federal Conservatives (unlike their provincial counterparts in Ontario, Alberta, and the Atlantic Provinces), having blown it so often, would blow it again. His task was to radiate confidence and competence, things that no Conservative leader had been able to combine since Sir Robert Borden had done in the First World War.

15

THE TAKEOVER

Whether he wins the job in an election, as Pierre Trudeau and Joe Clark did, or gets it as a bonus prize in the crackerjack box, à la John Turner, any new prime minister of Canada is in for some early shocks.

Trudeau's answer when he won re-election in 1980 was to turn his back on details, especially economic ones, and busy himself with great issues, like the Constitution and world peace.

Clark came to power in 1979 with great expectations, and promises of tax cuts and other goodies, including an undertaking that mortgage interest payments would become a tax credit.

But as soon as the books were opened and Clark took a look at the national accounts, he covered his eyes and moaned: "Oh, my God." The more the Conservatives pored over the mess, the worse it appeared to be, and all their brave proposals went into the trash can. When they finally dared bring in a budget, it was John Crosbie's "short-term pain for long-term gain," and the government was defeated on the issue of an 18-cent-a-gallon increase in the price of gasoline.

Trudeau got back in by fudging the issue and abolishing the gallon so nobody knew what they were paying for gasoline, except that it was twice as much as people were paying in the United States.

John Turner, entering the prime minister's office in 1984, encountered the same spectacle of horrors that greeted Joe Clark in 1979, except that for Turner, the gruesome details were so much worse.

The annual government deficit had tripled and was half again as great, proportionately, as that in the United States. Unemployment was double what it had been in 1979, and inflation was higher, and rising. Joe Clark had not had to cope with a 75-cent Canadian dollar, as Turner was called upon to do, thankful that most Canadians wouldn't remember how the Liberals defeated John Diefenbaker twenty-one years before because the Canadian dollar had sunk to 92 1/2 cents American.

For a man with a business background, it was a traumatic experience, especially as Turner's enemies kept saying he started the whole bloat of government deficits with his final budget of 1975. This was a load of guilt that he refused to shoulder, and when he looked around for someone to cling to, he could find no more reassuring figures than Trudeau's minister of finance, Marc Lalonde, and Lalonde's predecessor, Allan MacEachen. He insisted that they stay by him while he tried to tidy things up, putting on as brave a face as he could in public, and giving an appearance of openness with media that was a distinct contrast to Trudeau's lifelong contempt for the scribes and garglers of the national press corps.

"Howzat for open government, guys?" he quipped after one of his early scrums. It wasn't bad, even though what was being said out front had little relationship to what was going on behind the scenes, in Turner's Château Laurier suite where the new government was taking shape.

No sooner had John Turner been elected Liberal leader than he began to act as though he owned the place which, in a manner of speaking, he did.

He also acquired some outstanding obligations, quite apart from the problems facing the country and the party. There were accounts to be settled with Jean Chrétien, and with Pierre Trudeau, both of whom were in a mood, and a position, to be prickly.

In the two weeks between his election as Liberal leader and his swearing in as prime minister, Turner would have occasion to wonder why he had left the peace and security of the boardrooms for the political bazaar of Ottawa, taking a whopping pay cut in the process, and subjecting his family to the white light of publicity.

In the process, Geills Turner, once so dubious about politics, became Turner's biggest political asset, undertaking interviews and public appearances with every sign of enjoyment. At the swearing-in ceremony at Government House, she actually took on the massed forces of media at the front door while her husband slipped out the back, and she seemed ready to talk forever, insisting only that the broadcast reporters not thrust their microphones down her aristocratic throat.

For Turner, it was a time of wheeling and dealing. His prime adversaries were Chrétien, trading on his newly-expanded role as the most loved Liberal in Canada, and Trudeau, who was bent on using his terminal leverage to the full.

Chrétien was hanging tough on behalf not only of himself but of the people who had supported him during the leadership campaign and at the convention. Trudeau, in the oft-quoted words of poet Robert Frost, had promises to keep.

What resulted was some amazing political sleight-of-hand, and an unabashed plundering of the public purse as a legion of Liberals were installed at the trough, or given gilt-edged, signed-in-blood pledges of favours to come.

The dispensing of largesse, first by Trudeau and then by Trudeau and Turner combined, was so extreme that it brought howls of rage from two usually mild-mannered columnists, Jeffrey Simpson of the *Globe and Mail* and Richard Gwyn of the *Toronto Star*.

Simpson called it an orgy of patronage, a gravy train with all the Liberals waving from the windows, and Turner pushing and puffing from behind.

Gwyn called it a new, low watermark in standards of

political behaviour, and was undecided "whether to laugh or cry, to explode in rage or be sick." He talked about "not simply corruption, as is obvious, but of decadence."

Both Simpson and Gwyn aimed their barbs at the departing Trudeau, delivering only glancing blows at Turner while hoping he would move quickly to dispose of Trudeau's refuse—in particular, the rumoured appointments of two politicians to diplomatic posts, Eugene Whelan to Ireland and Bryce Mackasey to Portugal. Thus the way was open for Turner eventually to put some space between himself and Trudeau, something he had avoided doing at the convention but now wished heartily to do with all speed.

Trudeau's leverage over Turner was short-lived, but strong—if he rewarded all the members of parliament to whom he had promised rewards, he would denude the government benches and put the Liberal majority in jeopardy. This might not matter if an election would bring about the quick dissolution of the thirty-second Parliament, but it would limit Turner's options, which were few enough to begin with.

So the pork barrel came out and the distribution began, almost before the convention rubble in Ottawa's Civic Centre had been cleared away.

Mark MacGuigan was whisked onto the Federal Court bench, where he was joined by Government House Leader Yvon Pinard.

Onto the Canadian Transport Commission went John Munro.

Into the sanctuary of the Senate went Allan MacEachen, joined by Fisheries Minister Pierre De Bané and Public Works Minister Roméo LeBlanc, himself a former minister of fisheries. Former Trudeau aide and fishery prober Michael Kirby was already in the Senate, leading cynics to note that there was a stronger smell of fish in the Senate than in the outports.

That took care of three of Turner's convention opponents, MacGuigan, Munro, and Whelan, leaving three to be dealt with: Chrétien, Johnston, and Roberts. In the end, it was Chrétien himself who did the dealing, leading Turner to wonder who had won the leadership, anyway. In the back of his mind he had the knowledge that convention losers eventually fade away, even when they come close, as Robert Winters had come close to Trudeau in 1968.

Chrétien was unrelenting in his demands for himself and his supporters inside the new structure of government headed by Turner. He wanted the deputy prime minister-ship, a senior portfolio in the cabinet, and control over the patronage levers in Quebec, which have been in Liberal hands so long the handles are painted red.

His leverage was his threat to quit, thus cooling the ardour of all those Liberals who had said, and kept saying, how much they loved him.

MacEachen's resignation left two of the jobs vacant, secretary of state for external affairs and deputy prime minister, so Turner had no problem offering those to Chrétien. The Quebec patronage portfolio was more diffi-cult, because the inside track was held by the champion dispenser of political pork in Quebec, André Ouellet, and Ouellet had fought for Turner in Quebec and delivered a majority of Quebec delegates to him, giving Chrétien the coup-de-grace in the process.

Turner came up with a Solomon-like decision— Chrétien to be Number Two in Canada but Number One in Quebec, with Ouellet taking care of the domestic details as a member of a committee chaired by Chrétien. Ouellet agreed to be patient, and managed to smuggle an undistin-guished protégé of his into Turner's new cabinet, in the person of 28-year-old Jean Lapierre, the youngest cabinet minister in Canadian history.

The result was that Chrétien agreed to stay in the cabinet, thus giving the Liberals what Turner had promised them at the convention—elect me, and you'll get Chrétien, too. Except that it was a very uneasy and unsettled Chré-tien, forced now to keep to himself his views of Turner's Bay Street approach to government, so at odds with Chrétien's own Main Street concepts.

Meanwhile, back at the prime minister's office, Trudeau kept the appointments churning out, rewarding those who had been faithful to himself, and taking care of some of Chrétien's people who might find themselves neglected once Turner's hand was on the spigot.

A prime minister has at his disposal about 500 appointments to boards, commissions, corporations, and other arms of government, and these jobs range in tenure from three to ten years, pay being in the "range" between $50,000 and $100,000 a year, though the really fat ones can go as high as $250,000. The biggest plums of all, because they last until the incumbent is seventy or seventy-five, are appointments to the bench and to the Senate. Those appointed to the judiciary at least have the face-saving grace of having to work for their money, and arduous work it can be, requiring a special kind of intellect. Considering the way our judges are chosen, the remarkable thing is that justice is dispensed at all in our courts.

Turner himself has made much of the fact that he cleaned up the system of judicial appointments and took the patronage out of the system, yet it remains a fact that the vast proportion of federally appointed judges are former Grit bagmen or one-time candidates or just plain old hangers-on. This tradition continues in shameless fashion by the appointment to the Federal Court of Mark MacGuigan, who walked to Turner at the convention and was booed by the Chrétien faction, and Yvon Pinard, Trudeau's House leader who had never been cheered by anybody while in office, and was known chiefly for the computerized manner of his speech and the natty way he had of wearing Argyle knit sweaters.

Into the Senate, along with MacEachen, De Bané, and LeBlanc, went two Trudeau aides, Joyce Fairbairn and Colin Kenny, joining former Trudeau guru Michael Pitfield, the first top senior public servant ever given the Senate sinecure and the $61,400 that goes with it. Fairbairn would have thirty years of Senate service ahead of her, and Kenny would be there for 34 years, assuming the Senate lasts that long, a safe assumption.

Trudeau also gave Senate seats to Len Marchand, the

first Canadian Indian to sit in the Commons and in the cabinet, and Dan Hays, son of former Senator Harry Hays of Calgary.

Then he drew up his list of people to whom he had promised future favours, and got Turner to sign it, over Turner's objection that a simple gentleman's agreement would suffice.

That done, Trudeau headed off to the prime ministerial preserve at Harrington Lake, where Turner had granted him prolonged tenure, even as Joe Clark had done in 1979.

It was left to Turner to fit his new cabinet into the narrow confines he had set for himself, in his determination to reverse Parkinson's Law and cut back the numbers.

He had also promised news faces, and at least one of these was easy—his own, for Trudeau's.

Munro, MacGuigan, and Yvon Pinard were gone. Jean-Luc Pepin was sick, and out. Roméo LeBlanc and Pierre De Bané were in the Senate. Turner himself had no use for Pierre Bussières, Céline Hervieux-Payette and Jacques Olivier, three of Trudeau's ministers who had shown no capacity for office.

And Turner had resolved to have no unelected ministers in his cabinet—out went Bud Olson, Hazen Argue and Jack Austin, wiping out the representation of Alberta, Saskatchewan, and British Columbia in the cabinet, since there were no elected Liberal MPs from those provinces.

That meant thirteen of Trudeau's ministers gone, fourteen if Trudeau himself is counted. Twenty-three of the Trudeau ministers would stay, and with Turner himself installed, the size of the cabinet was below the goal of twenty-eight that Turner had set himself.

But what about the new faces he had promised?

Chrétien's was an old and very essential face. Having persuaded Allan MacEachen to stay as government leader in the Senate, Turner prevailed on Marc Lalonde to stick around as well, as minister of finance. And Herb Gray would remain as president of the Treasury Board. Other familiar holdovers were André Ouellet, Monique Bégin, Jean-Jacques Blais, Francis Fox, Gerald Regan, Ed Lumley, Dave Smith, and Roy MacLaren. Lloyd Axworthy was solid, representing the entire western component of the cabinet.

Nothing fresh in that bunch. Chrétien insisted that John Roberts be kept on, a payoff for Roberts' support in the second convention ballot. Bob Kaplan had enough ethnic and financial clout to hang onto the solicitor general's portfolio, and William Rompkey was the only appointable minister from Newfoundland, even though Trudeau had once fired him. Don Johnston emerged from the convention taller than he went in, and deserved a top job, but not finance.

Judy Erola would stay, her presence beefed up to compensate for the firing of Hervieux-Payette.

For his new faces, Turner did a couple of unexpected things, bringing in Doug Frith to be minister of Indian affairs and northern development, and Jean Lapierre as youth minister responsible for fitness and amateur sport.

What was unusual about Frith was that he came from Sudbury, like Judy Erola—and including North Bay's Jean-Jacques Blais, that gave Northern Ontario three ministers in a cabinet with no representation at all from three western provinces and none from the Quebec City area.

The thing about Lapierre was that, at twenty-eight, he was the youngest cabinet minister in Canadian history, with no record of achievement, dependent on André Ouellet's sponsorship for his claim to high office. There was the additional fact that his riding of Shefford bordered the riding in which Brian Mulroney was thinking about running, offering the prospect of an anti-Mulroney blitz of patronage.

The Liberal whip in the House of Commons, Charles Turner, was so surprised at the Frith and Lapierre appointments that he nearly swallowed his teeth. From his home in London, Turner, himself in line for one of the delayed-action Senate appointments, said neither man deserved promotion because "they were never there when I wanted them." He said the moral seemed to be that the less an MP does, the better the prospects for cabinet appointment.

Charles Turner thought more highly of John Turner's

choice of Ralph Ferguson as agriculture minister, and Herb Breau as minister of fisheries and oceans, saying both were hard workers.

The final new face was that of Rémi Bujold, who had co-chaired the leadership convention with Iona Campagnolo.

At the swearing-in of the cabinet, Mrs. Campagnolo said she herself would be running for election in British Columbia, and Turner quickly followed suit by saying that he, too, would run in B.C. Those two announcements made more news, as it turned out, than the composition of the "new" cabinet.

His inner cabinet—the planning and priorities committee—would be all old faces, except for Turner himself and an expanded role for Ed Lumley. The others were Chrétien, Roberts, Johnston, MacEachen, Lalonde, Gray, Ouellet, Regan, Axworthy, and Erola.

His makeshift housekeeping done, Turner proceeded to take a look at the state of the economy, and the state of the public opinion polls, and when he punched all the figures into the computer, the answer came up—go now. Right now.

By the end of his first week in office, he was off to London to visit the Queen, armed with a Gallup Poll taken after the leadership convention, showing him with an 11-point bulge over Mulroney.

16

ELECTION, 1984

In the second half of the twentieth century, Canada had held eleven federal elections, but never one like the election of 1984.

Two new and untried leaders were facing one another for the first time, something that hadn't happened since Louis St. Laurent's Liberals faced George Drew's Tories in 1949.

Almost five years had elapsed since the previous election was forced by a vote in the House of Commons, late in 1979. That was a long time between elections for a country that had known six elections between 1957 and 1968, and four elections between 1972 and 1980.

In fifty years, the Conservatives had ten leaders, three of whom became prime minister for brief periods. Over the same period, the Liberals had five leaders, all of whom came to power, Mackenzie King winning five mandates and Pierre Trudeau four.

What was different about this election was not just the newness of John Turner and Brian Mulroney, nor even the fact that both of them brought business backgrounds to high political office for the first time.

Both had come to leadership under contentious circumstances.

Mulroney had set himself to displace Joe Clark as

Conservative leader, and he succeeded, inflicting yet another in a long series of splits on the party. That he managed to piece the party back together and hold it in place for the year leading upto the election, put him in a class by himself, by comparison with previous Tory leaders.

John Turner had been PM-in-waiting for years in Pierre Trudeau's first three cabinets, but there was tension between the two that grew into active distaste and distrust, to the point where Turner quit party and politics in 1975, throwing his riding to the Tory wolves and going off to make his pile as a corporate lawyer in Toronto. From that moment, it was part of Trudeau's objective to prevent Turner from ever becoming Liberal leader or prime minister.

Turner's accomplishment was to keep his name in the minds of Liberals through the last ten years of Trudeau, to the point where the leadership fell into his lap when it became impossible for Trudeau to stay on. It was the first time in the century that the Liberal leadership passed between two men who hated one another, and yet Turner, like Mulroney, preserved at least an outward semblance of party unity, while washing his hands of Trudeau and all his works.

Turner also managed to take his party into the election as slight favourites in the polls, despite high unemployment, rising interest rates, a 75-cent dollar, and annual deficits that were eating huge holes in government revenues and imposing debt loads that would make financial cripples out of future generations of Canadians, on top of the burdens they would face sustaining the social programs and the expanding load of aging Canadians.

Two of the most physically attractive men ever to enter Canadian politics were facing one another for the top office in the land. Canadians had often complained that their best people didn't enter politics, but here we had at least two of the best-looking ones.

There was no reason, of course, to believe that Canadians preferred good-looking politicians. Starting with Sir

John A. Macdonald, a series of homely men had governed the country, Sir Wilfrid Laurier being the exception, together with such courtly specimens as Sir Robert Borden and Louis St. Laurent, about whom there was nothing sexy. Mackenzie King was as uninspiring in appearance as he was in speech. John Diefenbaker, like Jean Chrétien, could contort his features until he resembled Frankenstein's monster, and Lester Pearson was so undistinctive in appearance he had to wear a bow tie to sort himself out from the crowd. Joe Clark was likened to Howdy Doody, and Robert Stanfield to an undertaker, or even Quasimodo. Pierre Trudeau, the sexiest prime minister Canada ever had, was not handsome in the classic, Turner/Mulroney sense of the word, with his pockmarked, skull-shaped face, high cheekbones, thinning hair, and slanty eyes. It was the way Trudeau put it all together that made him distinctive, and his mobile features and skittish mind could put together as many as thirty-six changes of expression and mood, by actual count.

John Turner projected the boardroom look, in the best Hollywood typecasting mode—you could smell prosperity on him, and an expensive upbringing, just as you could on his wife, Geills.

Brian Mulroney had one feature that Joe Clark conspicuously lacked, a chin. A massive chin. An absurdly prominent chin, giving him a profile like that of the old Duke of Wellington, who himself was the model for Punchinello and the Man in the Moon. To go with the chin he had a deep, bedroom voice, as opposed to Turner's crisp boardroom tones. And Mulroney sported Walter Pidgeon eyebrows, positioned on his Irish face in an attitude of prayer, peaking above his ample nose and his narrow mouth. To go with all this was a sense of humour, shared in full by the beautiful Mila Mulroney.

NDP Leader Ed Broadbent scoffed that Turner and Mulroney were the Bobbsey Twins of Bay Street, and he talked about *Brian* Turner and *John* Mulroney, but in fact there were deep differences between the two, as the summer election campaign would show.

The date of the election, September 4, was no surprise. But surprising, indeed, were Turner's and Mulroney's choices of the ridings in which they themselves would seek election. Turner picked British Columbia, the first Liberal leader and the first incumbent prime minister ever to do so. Mulroney picked rural Quebec, another first for a major party leader. It may have been that neither man had a choice, since Turner had set himself to revive the Liberal Party in Western Canada, and Mulroney's task was to win some Quebec seats for the Tories.

Both men described their choices as "homecomings." Turner had gone to university in Vancouver, and could equally have claimed other places as home—Montreal, Ottawa, Toronto. Mulroney grew up in Baie Comeau, but left there to attend university in Antigonish, Nova Scotia, and Quebec City. When it came to making his fortune, his base was Montreal, and when he finally came to run for Parliament, he chose the Down East riding of Central Nova.

But for the showdown, it was back to his roots in Manicuagan, the place of his youth, and the domain that he had administered as president of the Iron Ore Company of Canada, in the course of which he had to preside over the closing of the mining town of Schefferville. The riding was a long-time Liberal stronghold, and of the two gambles, Mulroney's and Turner's, Mulroney's was the more daring.

Both men were working without safety nets, and it was widely assumed that the loser would lose everything—the election, his leadership, the chance at a place in history.

Both carried handicaps into the campaign, and Turner's was Trudeau—the Trudeau years, which he was at pains to note he had not shared after 1975. Trudeau saddled him with an incredible list of patronage appointments, some of which Turner had to make himself, having bound himself to do so in a written agreement.

This earned him the scorn not only of his opponents, but brought down on his head a shower of media abuse the likes of which he had not had to endure thus far in his return to politics.

"Turner struggles to disown Trudeau," headlined the

Montreal Gazette at the end of the first campaign week, and
I was moved to recall Josef Stalin's legacy to his successor
in the Soviet Union, consisting of two letters, one to be
opened a year after Stalin's death, the other at the end of
the second year.

When a hard-pressed Nikita Khrushchev opened the
first letter, he read two words: "Blame me."

Khrushchev did, and in the resulting turmoil things got
better for a while, but after twelve months the rot set in
again and Khrushchev grabbed for the second letter. It
read: "Do as I did."

Trudeau's memory was too fresh for Turner to blame
him, and yet time was too short for Turner to make his own
mark—so he had to settle for putting what distance he
could between himself and Trudeau. The biggest embar-
rassment was Trudeau's nomination of Bryce Mackasey to
be ambassador to Portugal, a gaffe made worse by the fact
that the Portuguese government was not consulted in
advance. Asked if he supported the Mackasey appointment, Turner could make only the lame response that
"well, he's our candidate."

Mulroney's handicap was of a different kind. Having
had a year in which to make his own impression on the
Canadian people, he had fallen back from his 1983 popularity peak by seeming to be short of original ideas. He defied
elements of his own party by supporting the Trudeau
government's initiatives on the Manitoba language question and on medicare, but he got few high marks for
courage and a lot of low ones for being a "closet liberal."

When he opened his treasure chest of election promises and poured out his policies for economic recovery,
John Crosbie gave the media a peek at a document purport-
ing to show that the Tory promises would cost $20 million
to keep, over five years. Crosbie, whose "short-term pain
for long-term gain" 1979 budget had cost the life of the Joe
Clark government, seemed to be at it again, and it was
another case of the truth blocking the road to power. It was
the same Down East syndrome that had wrecked Robert
Stanfield's chances in 1974, when he talked economic
sense to the Canadian people and got clobbered.

Mulroney fudged the books and soldiered on, saying he would talk about costs later in the campaign, which put him on the same footing as Turner, who was also hedging on the balance sheet, acting and talking like a man who wanted to get the election over as quickly as possible so he could commence the unpopular measures that would be needed to reverse the downward drift.

As a counter to Crosbie's damaging realism, Mulroney had the expressed support not only of Joe Clark but of all the Conservative premiers, notably William Davis of Ontario, who had put his entire electoral machine, known as the "Big Blue," at Mulroney's disposal. It was a disposition greatly to be cherished.

The decision having been made for a summer election, Her Majesty declined Turner's suggestion that her July tour take place anyway, since it was entirely a provincial affair involving New Brunswick, Ontario, and Manitoba. But she said she would be glad to come after the Pope had left in September, since she had a private trip scheduled anyway to visit thoroughbred stud farms in the United States.

Turner flew home in his Canadair Challenger jet, which in some circles was itself regarded as a piece of bravado. As soon as he returned, he made the election announcement, along with the balance of the patronage appointments Trudeau had made him agree to. Turner said he had put the appointments off until the last minute because so many of them involved sitting Liberal MPs, and if they had been rewarded earlier, the Liberal majority in the House of Commons would have been lost, and Governor General Jeanne Sauvé might have denied him dissolution, summoning Mulroney.

This was the first enormous piece of nonsense of the campaign, and there were more pieces to follow. Former Senator Eugene Forsey said Turner's excuse for accepting Trudeau's delayed-action patronage appointments was palpable nonsense, and suggested Turner's advisers needed to have their heads examined.

As it turned out, it was Turner whose judgement was most in question, and the outcry over misuse of patronage spread from the pundits and opposition spokesmen to the public at large.

Trudeau, it seemed, had dealt Turner a grave blow at the outset of his mandate, whether deliberately or by chance—most people thought the former. Both Brian Mulroney and NDP Leader Ed Broadbent took off with the issue and were clobbering the Grits with it when Mulroney, under the continuing impression that members of the media corps were his pals, let his hair down on the campaign plane.

He told members of his travelling media troupe that he himself had promised patronage to Conservatives during last year's leadership race, because that was what Tories wanted to hear. And commenting on the infamous appointment of Bryce Mackasey as Canadian ambassador to Portugal, he said: "Let's face it, there's no whore like an old whore. If I'd been in Bryce's position, I'd have been right in there with my nose in the public trough like all the rest of them."

Two days later, Mulroney admitted in Sault Ste. Marie that he had made a mistake, and that he regretted saying what he had said under the impression that he was off the record. Any politician who talks to media people, singly or en masse, on the assumption that there will be no reporting, is clearly lacking in common sense, and so Mulroney's savvy took a beating, putting at risk what might have been the most telling election issue, handed to the Tories on a plate by the departing Trudeau, with Turner's weak-kneed acquiesence.

Apart from the patronage issue, the opening weeks of the campaign were marked by intense airborne campaigning by Broadbent and Mulroney, and a slow start by Turner. Both Turner and Mulroney unveiled proposed New Deals for Western Canada, and each accused the other of policy theft. All parties agreed on a new approach to the National Energy Policy.

Turner unveiled his slate of candidates in Quebec, minus the old stars, Trudeau, Marc Lalonde, and Monique Bégin. Mulroney introduced his own candidates in Quebec, short on stars but quicker off the mark than the Liberals.

The encouraging thing to the Conservatives was that so many people wanted to run for them in Quebec and so many people showed up for Conservative nomination meetings. But the polls still showed the Liberals with more than double the support of the Tories in Quebec.

Turner's biggest gamble involved his own candidacy. He decided to run in the riding of Vancouver Quadra, a Tory seat since 1972. Mulroney responded by announcing he would run in the Quebec riding of Manicouagan, the easternmost region of Quebec, bordering Labrador, where no Conservative had ever been elected.

In the early going, the man with most to be concerned about seemed to be Jean Chrétien, who had undertaken a quick round-the-world tour as soon as Turner named him external affairs minister. Chrétien was away when the election was called, and he returned with a severe case of dysentery and fatigue, causing his doctor to recommend a rest. As a result, Chrétien missed Turner's big Montreal press conference at which his "new look" slate of candidates was introduced, and he read in the papers the suggestion that former Quebec finance minister Raymond Garneau would be Turner's new Quebec "star." This, plus the fact that the Turner team proposed to have Chrétien campaign almost entirely in English-speaking Canada, seemed to signal that Chrétien's time as "Number Two in Canada, Number One in Quebec" might not last long after the election, whether the Liberals won or lost.

Mulroney tried to keep the patronage issue sputtering by coming up with a figure of $80 million, describing that as the cost to the taxpayers for the mass of patronage appointments. The Liberals kept throwing his own patronage promises at him, leading Mulroney to take what I described as the vow of chastity, saying in effect that, if he won the election, all his own appointments to trough posts would be on the basis of merit, rather than party service.

The most vigorous argument of the early campaign was over whether or not to hold television debates, and if so, when. Turner held firm for two early debates, one in French and one in English, and he got his way, whereupon he took a week off from campaigning.

17

THE DECLINE

What followed was a political spectacle unlike anything seen before in Canada, or anywhere else for that matter.

Parallels would be drawn between the campaign of Republican candidate for president Thomas E. Dewey in 1948, when Harry Truman nipped him at the wire. But there was to be nothing nippy about what was in store for John Turner and the Liberals.

Defeat, it seemed, had been in the cards all along.

Perhaps there had been no cards at all, and what Pierre Trudeau had handed to Turner was an empty deck.

Perhaps the shortcomings of the Liberal election campaign were Turner's own. He himself, when he entered the Liberal leadership race, had worried that he was not the man his supporters believed him to be, and that he would not be equal to the challenge.

Or perhaps the real cause of the decline and fall of the Liberal Party was Brian Mulroney himself, engineering a political coup that would make him the biggest winner ever, and Turner the biggest loser.

The tendency to blame it all on Trudeau was the one that would find most favour with most Liberals, who would trace their woes back to 1979 and the defeat in Parliament of the Joe Clark government, followed by Trudeau's withdrawal of his resignation and his decision to contest the 1980 election.

By thus undertaking a fourth mandate as prime minister, Trudeau stretched his own time in office to historic proportions, but he also used up his own and the Liberal Party's credit with the Canadian people. He grew careless about his homework, playing more and more the statesman and less and less the politician, while the economy went to pot.

In Trudeau's final years the party machinery rusted away, to the point that when John Turner tried to get the wheels moving, they fell off.

In political legend, this would be known as Trudeau's revenge—a case of vindictive neglect to ensure that when the hated Turner achieved the Liberal leadership, he would fall on his face.

There would be truth in most of this, and it would give weight to the Liberal explanation that what ruined them was the public's conviction that it was time for a change, and that twenty-one years of Grit rule under Pearson and Trudeau were enough.

By this reckoning, no new leader could have won the 1984 election for the Liberals, and the party would have met the same fate under Jean Chrétien as under John Turner.

Doubtless Mulroney would have won in any event, but it is hard to imagine Liberal support in Quebec caving in on Chrétien the way it did on Turner.

Added to the "time for a change" syndrome was Turner's own performance as a campaigner, confounding the bill of goods sold to Liberal convention delegates that he was a supreme manager and a sure winner. Turner might complain that Trudeau had done him dirty, but he proceeded to cover himself with additional soot and grime and, before the campaign was over, sleaze.

As for the Mulroney factor, the credit for brilliant management was all his—a party machine running full tilt from the moment of Trudeau's February resignation announcement, a battle plan that was followed with scarcely a change to a victory that reduced the Liberal Party to tatters, and shattered the Grit power base in Quebec.

Trudeau's departure opened the eyes and ears of Quebeckers, and the man they saw and heard was Mulroney, calling them to the vision of a new and united Canada.

Turner, the darling of the media during the Liberal leadership convention, quickly became the goat, receiving the same treatment that had been handed out to Joe Clark in 1979. The impression was one of incompetence, and the more Turner tried to shake it, the worse it got.

The result was one of the few election campaigns that visibly influenced public opinion, the apparent winner at the start emerging as a total loser at the end.

Perhaps, as Brian Mulroney insisted, it was all pre-ordained—but there could be no doubt that the TV debates of July 23 and 24 marked the turning point and that, for John Turner, it was all downhill from there.

The skid had started before the debates, because of the patronage issue which, instead of being forgotten as Turner had hoped, continued to fester, rubbed raw by Mulroney.

Then there was the amazing business of the bum patting, Turner having been caught by the cameras delivering a whack on what he himself described as Party President Iona Campagnolo's "perfect ass." She gave him a clout in return, on what were known in the jock set as the tightest buns in the business, a reference to Turner's tense style of walking.

A national furore resulted in advance of the TV debates, with photographs of women wearing "bum wraps" to protect themselves, and Turner defending himself as a very tactile guy, and women's groups erupting in indignation, some of it coming from inside the Liberal camp.

Turner kept insisting that the issue was meaningless, and in doing so he sounded more and more out of touch with one of the realities of the 1980s, the emergence of women into equal partnership, or at least the beginnings of it.

It would be twenty-three days before Turner would apologize for his gesture—twenty-four days in which the word "bum" became part of everyday Canadian vocabulary, always with Turner's hand attached.

In vain did Geills Turner insist that her husband was not a bottom pincher. Turner's efforts to turn the debate into what he called more serious channels only played up the fact that he did not regard the handling of women's posteriors as being anything more serious than a handshake or a peck on the cheek.

So much for the thought that the departure of that old sex symbol, Pierre Trudeau, would take the outrageous element out of our politics.

Turner's bum patting proclivities made the *New York Times* and the *Wall Street Journal*, with lengthy clips about it on the major American TV networks.

The Liberals put out a code of conduct for candidates, urging men and women to touch one another, but not feel.

One of the authors of that code was Turner's colleague Judy Erola, the flying Finn who was headed for defeat in her home riding of Nickel Belt. Having issued her instructions on decorum between the genders, she then joined Finance Minister Marc Lalonde in an announcement that sanitary napkins and tampons would be exempted from the federal sales tax, retroactive to March 23, a four-month kickback for users. Erola said her consumer and corporate affairs department would monitor the impact of this removal on the consumer price for those products.

Lalonde said the products were essential for women, something the TV ads had been emphasizing since the invention of the tube. But this was the first time the products had figured in an election pitch for votes.

On the wires of the usually staid Canadian Press, we were informed under the byline of the usually stern-penned Juliet O'Neill that following the nomination of Geraldine Ferraro to be Fritz Mondale's running mate for the Democrats, lapel buttons appeared at the San Francisco convention touting ''Fritz and Tits.''

Editorial cartoonists had a ball.

The *Ottawa Citizen* portrayed the bottoms of Iona Campagnolo and another of Turner's ''pats,'' Lisa St. Martin Tremblay, with big hand prints on them.

Tremblay was quoted as saying Trudeau was cool, but Turner was hot.

Grit candidate Lucie Pepin said Turner had better cut it out, but explained to her Quebec constituents that Anglophones always go around hitting each other on the derrières.

Assorted Anglophones wondered where they had been all their lives, but lacked the nerve to start whacking.

The good, grey *Globe and Mail* showed a Canada goose in full flight, with Turner's hand where its head should be.

The *Toronto Sun* pictured Turner wearing handcuffs.

Newspapers everywhere carried photographs of women wearing bum wraps, and the big item in Ottawa was a traffic sign, depicting the rear view of a man and a woman, and the man had his hand on the woman's rump, and the scene had a diagonal line slashed through it, the international symbol for "no."

NDP Leader Ed Broadbent said his daughter turned thumbs down on Turner patting women's backsides, claiming the practice was a relic of an earlier generation—mine, presumably, though I don't remember back beyond the yo-yo craze.

Mila Mulroney said it was rotten, and that Turner had better not try to pat hers.

Turner said his moves came naturally and that "it's tangible, it's tactile, it's face to face, *mano a mano.*" The suggestion was made that Turner needed an Italian dictionary if he thought "*mano a mano*" translated into "hand on bottom." Italians pointed out that their custom didn't involve patting women's bums. They pinch them.

My favourite female cousin, seventy-four-year-old Mary Louise Lynch, long-time stalwart member of the National Parole Board and hence familiar with the racier side of society, said the prime minister could whack her derrière any time without causing offence. And she was a lifetime Tory.

In New Brunswick, Mr. Justice J.C. Angers ruled that a women's breasts were a secondary sexual characteristic, similar to a man's whiskers. And my own son, Judge C. Blake Lynch of Fredericton, ruled that the learned justice was out of touch with the realities of life, and that massaging a woman's breasts without her consent constituted sexual assault. My son's views were aired across the land and he became a hero with the women's lobby.

In the midst of all this, the women's lobby demanded, and got, a debate by the three party leaders on women's issues, which shaped up as a dandy.

Ed Broadbent would have the edge with his proposal for a 42 per cent quota of women on jobs created under special federal government programs, and his support of equal pay for work of equal value, across the board.

Judy Erola was exulting that she and Monique Bégin had accomplished a total conversion of John Turner on women's issues, insisting that he not only knew the words, he could sing the music, too.

And just sixteen years had passed since Judy LaMarsh, on national television, had been caught calling Trudeau "that bastard."

Apart from bums, the week before the television debates was enlivened by three events that would reverberate through the rest of the campaign.

John Crosbie, who had been minister of finance in the Clark government and Mulroney's rival for the leadership in 1983, let slip a document that seemed to say it would cost $20 million over five years to fulfil Mulroney's election promises.

Crosbie did nothing to stifle the resultant commotion, and the Liberals, who earlier had scorned Mulroney for making no promises at all, jumped on the issue and made it central to all their campaign speeches and pamphlets.

Mulroney disavowed the figure, but would return to the issue later. Meanwhile, there was speculation that the Tories might try to muffle the voice of Crosbie, one of their most popular public speakers—and certainly, little was heard from him nationally for the balance of the campaign.

The third event was the wholehearted entry into the campaign of Ontario Premier William Davis, in support of Mulroney's candidacy. Davis had long before turned over his provincial campaign apparatus to Mulroney, who had accepted it holus bolus, building his own national apparatus on the foundation of Davis' "Big Blue Machine."

There were howls from the Liberals and New Democrats that Davis had Mulroney on a leash, and there were cries of protest from federal Tories, including some of Mulroney's long-time intimates, who found themselves being shouldered aside by Norman Atkins and his crew of slick operatives from Toronto. But politics, Mulroney kept saying, was the art of the possible, and with good organization, everything was possible if you just believed.

Mulroney believed, and his organization saw to it that he was superbly briefed in advance of the TV debates, while John Turner was torn right up to air time by the conflicting views he was getting from his assorted advisers.

The debates were to settle John Turner's hash, though he would not know what hit him until later. The downward turn for Turner would be matched by an upturn for Mulroney, and a complete reversal of fortunes for the New Democrats and their leader, Ed Broadbent, who had been wallowing at an all-time low in the public opinion polls, fearing a wipe-out on election day.

Broadbent gained good marks merely for showing up on July 24 for the French-language debate, and for expressing himself as fluently as he did in the other official language.

Turner got bad marks for being uptight and for indecisive answers on the language laws of Quebec and Manitoba, subjects on which he had earlier issued a series of "clarifications."

The big winner was Mulroney—looking, sounding, shrugging, laughing, frowning for all the world like a Quebecker, speaking the lingo, quick on the draw, every word accenting his own Quebec origins and identity. That was the start of what came to be called the "Tory Blue Thunder" in Quebec, and all across French Canada from Acadia to St. Boniface. Lightning was more like it.

The English-language debate the following night was almost as devastating for Turner, and as successful for Mulroney, with Broadbent gaining points of his own from the equal time he was accorded.

It is not often that we can point to a single moment, or even a single issue, that marked the turning point of a campaign—perhaps C.D. Howe's "what's a million?" in 1957, or Lester Pearson's endorsement of nuclear weapons in 1963, or the Clark-Crosbie budget's "short-term pain for long-term gain" in 1979. Perhaps, too, Trudeau's crucifixion of Robert Stanfield in 1974 with the words, "zap, you're frozen!"

In the 1984 campaign, certainly as far as English-speaking Canadians were concerned, the turning point came toward the end of the two hours when, to the horror of his supporters and the delight of his opponents, Turner himself brought up the issue of patronage, which had inflicted such damage on his campaign from its outset. The subsequent exchange between Turner and Mulroney has been classed as everything from great television to political suicide. In fact, it was both.

Turner: We have this patronage issue brought up early. Mr. Mulroney has not been dealing with that issue in the same way. He told his party last year that he was going to ensure that every available job would be made available to every living, breathing Conservative. You know, I have these facts right here. I can give you this quote which comes from the *Montreal Gazette*, May 18, 1983—"Oh, there will be jobs for Liberals and NDPers too, but only after I have been prime minister for fifteen years and I can't find a single, living, breathing Tory to appoint." And when accosted with that statement, Mr. Mulroney said, "Well, you know, you have to treat the party faithful one way, but now we have an election and I am talking differently to Canadians."

Mulroney: I beg your pardon, sir.

Turner: You said that; then you said you were just joking last night, but that is not a joking matter.

Mulroney: No, it is not a joking matter, sir, but you have raised this issue of patronage tonight. You have done something that has never been done before. You have appointed nineteen in one of the most remarkable acts, and I think it is generally recognized as a really quite remarkable act of appointing nineteen Liberal members at the last second in a secret deal with a letter which you have yet to produce to the Canadian people. I made those statements in the full light of day during a leadership campaign. I made them as someone who has never made a political appointment in my life. I am a member of a political party. I have never benefitted from one.

The Liberals have made all of the thousands of appointments over the last two decades or so, here in Ottawa. Sure, from time to time I will acknowledge it and I have apologized for it. I apologized for it and perhaps that is what you should have done, sir, for having made them in the first place. But I acknowledge that, that I said that, with a smile, and it was captured by the television cameras during the course of the debate. But the fact of the matter is, sir, that you took a secret arrangement and you honoured it on behalf of a political party, I think to the detriment of Canada.

Turner: I am just saying to you, Mr. Mulroney, that I say the same thing to my party publicly as I say to Canadians.

Mulroney: So do I.

(Moments later)

Mulroney: The appointments which we discussed earlier, I think, confirm the fact that it's the "old boy" network back in town; that the boys are back and the Liberal Party doesn't want change.

Turner: I would say, Mr. Mulroney, that on the basis of what you have talked about—putting your nose in the public trough—that you wouldn't offer Canadians any newness in the style of government. The style that you have been preaching to your own party reminds me of the old Union Nationale. It reminds me of patronage at its best. Frankly, on the basis of your performance, I cannot see freshness coming out of your choice.

Mulroney: Mr. Turner, the only person who has ever been appointed around here for the last twenty-odd years has been by your party, and 99 per cent of them have been Liberals, and you ought not to be proud of that, nor should you repeat something that I think you know to be inaccurate.

You know full well that that was a figure of speech that

was used, and I do not deny it. In fact, I have gone so far, because I believe what you did was so bad, I have gone so far, sir, as to apologize for even kidding about it. I have apologized to the Canadian people for kidding about it. The least you should do is apologize for having made these horrible appointments. I have had the decency, I think, to acknowledge that I was wrong in even kidding about it. I shouldn't have done that, and I said so. You, sir, at least owe the Canadian people a profound apology for doing it . . .

I say to you, sir, two things. You should produce that letter because you keep coming back to this situation. Please produce the secret letter that you signed when you undertook to make these appointments.

May I say respectfully that, if I felt I owed the Canadian people—and I did—an apology for bantering about the subject you, sir, owe the Canadian people a deep apology for having indulged in that kind of practice with those kinds of appointments.

Turner: Well, I have told you and told the Canadian people, Mr. Mulroney, that I had no option.

Mulroney: You had an option, sir. You could have said, "I am not going to do it. This is wrong for Canada, and I am not going to ask Canadians to pay the price." You had an option, sir, to say no, and you chose to say yes to the old attitudes and the old stories of the Liberal Party. That, sir, if I may say respectfully, that is not good enough for Canadians.

Turner: I had no option. I was . . .

Mulroney: That is an avowal of failure. That is a confession of non-leadership and this country needs leadership. You had an option, sir. You could have done better.

Moderator: Mr. Turner, your response, please.

Turner: I just said, Mr. Moderator, taking the Canadian people through the circumstances, Mr. Trudeau had every right to make those appointments before he resigned. In order that he do so, yes, I had to make a commitment to him. Otherwise I was advised that, with serious consequences to the Canadian people, I could not have been granted the opportunity of forming a government.

Moderator: Next question, please.

End of exchange. End of election. End of the image that had carried John Turner to the leadership of his party.

Brian Mulroney lifted Turner's words verbatim from the tapes of the debate and made them the keystone of every speech he made from one end of the country to the other, for the duration of the campaign.

The words became so familiar, through newspaper reports and broadcasts, that audiences came to expect them, and even to clamour for him to do what came to be known as "the devil bit," helped by a news photo of Turner, wearing a Satanic expression, with two forks protruding from his head.

The punchline came when Mulroney imitated Turner saying, in a high falsetto: "But I had no option!"

There would be a long pause, and Mulroney would raise his eyes to heaven, continuing in a quavering voice: "The devil made me do it!"

Thus Mulroney skewered Trudeau and Turner in a single phrase from comedian Flip Wilson, and it convulsed the crowds, along with Mulroney's mockery of Turner for sending so many of his friends to "Grit heaven," and for running a lottery in which Eugene Whelan won first prize, a trip to Rome.

Prior to the two TV debates, Turner had agreed to a third, to be held on August 15, on women's issues.

That debate would produce nothing like the on-air drama recounted above, but it would be a bonanza for Broadbent, whose party was so closely involved with women's issues that it could claim to have discovered them.

Broadbent entered the August 15 debate a hero with the live crowd of women that was on hand, and with groups of women watching the telecast across the country. He drew cheers and applause, while Turner and especially Mulroney were booed and hissed for hedging on complete equality of gender in the workplace, both in the public and private sectors, and for indicating the complexities involved in the pledge of "equal pay for work of equal value."

The debates produced a loser in Turner, with both Mulroney and Broadbent picking up a share of the pieces. Broadbent got the biggest share, certainly with the women, but it was Mulroney who would triumph most resoundingly in the end, his party winding up with seventeen women MPs in the new Parliament.

For Turner, as perhaps for all incumbents facing an election, the lesson seemed to be to shun all TV debates, not only because of the pitfalls and pratfalls they present, but also because the equal time provisions give equal stature to opposition leaders—"equal exposure for unequal representation."

Curiously, neither of the major parties had quibbled about the New Democrats having the same share of debate time as the Liberals and Conservatives, thus handing Broadbent an opportunity that money could not buy. It remained for him to make the most of it, and in the process double his party's standing in the public opinion polls, safeguarding his own leadership at the same time. The NDP passed from the spectre of oblivion to the prospect of replacing the Liberals as the official opposition in the House of Commons.

The debate, more than any other factor, convinced Canadians that the big election winners would be the Conservatives—a prospect soon to be confirmed by the swing in the public opinion polls. And that, in turn, relieved whatever alarm voters might have felt about a Parliament in which the New Democrats would have had the balance of power, repeating their high spending antics of the 1972 minority Parliament, when they enjoyed power without responsibility.

The growing certainty of a Conservative majority, trumpeted by polls and pundits alike, would take the steam out of Mulroney's argument, in NDP ridings, that "if you vote for the New Democrats, you're going to get the Liberals, ten times out of ten." Obviously, that wasn't going to happen this time, nor would NDP MPs have another chance to unite with the Liberals, as they had done in 1979, to throw the Tories out and restore the Grits to power.

So the NDP came back from the abyss, doubling the

party's standing in most of the polls, from a low of 10 to a high of 20.

For John Turner, there was no such comfort.

In the debate of July 25, Broadbent had said that Manitoba, with its NDP government, "has an absolutely terrific record, in the past year, of promoting jobs."

Turner, glancing down at one of his briefing papers, countered that "one of the reasons Manitoba has a lower unemployment rate these days is that it is exporting 2,000 people a month out of the province of Manitoba into other parts of the country, and into other parts of this continent."

Broadbent made no response, but Premier Howard Pawley of Manitoba was quick the next day to call Turner a liar.

Turner, checking the figures that had been fed him by campaign co-chairman Izzy Asper of Winnipeg, found they were wrong. Manitoba was gaining population, not losing it.

Turner apologized five days later, praising Pawley's sensible approach to good government.

By now, Turner was on a one-way trip on the down escalator, with the vultures of media pecking at him without mercy, as they had at Joe Clark for lost luggage and falling on bayonets and promising to move the Canadian embassy from Tel Aviv to Jerusalem.

The name they hung on Clark was "wimp." On Turner, it was "bumbler"—the same tag United States media had hung on President Gerry Ford a decade earlier, from which Ford never recovered. The damage to Turner, as registered at the voting booths, would be much deeper.

On July 27, Gallup issued a poll that was conducted before Turner called the summer election. It showed the Liberals leading in popular support, but with 38 per cent of respondents undecided.

Before it finished, this would be the most-polled and most-analysed election ever held in Canada, and there would be demands for the suppression of polls, and denials from the pollsters that their figures influenced the thinking of voters.

One things was sure, the polls influenced the thinking of reporters and commentators, to the extent that from July 27, the poll figures, particularly those of Gallup, CTV, CBC, and Southam, made the biggest headlines of the campaign, dominated the largest of the TV specials, and set the tone for coverage of the final five weeks of the election. For John Turner, it was a tone of torment that was to drive him, his wife, and his advisers to distraction, and dejection.

On July 28, Turner stepped on a banana peel again, and this time it was one he should have seen and avoided. The wretched briefing papers contained a typographical error, and Turner read it out verbatim, quoting Mulroney as saying that when elected, he would fire 600,000 civil servants.

The awful thing about that howler is that Mulroney could fire every federal civil servant in the country and still be about 150,000 shy of Turner's total. So Turner apologized again for misquotation.

In this case, the mistake was unforgiveable in a man who has gained the prime ministership of his country and is seeking ratification by the voters. If he doesn't have the faintest ballpark idea of the size of the federal public service, what does he know?

People began wondering what it was in Turner that had made him such a success on Bay Street and had brought so many directorships his way. Could it be that the man couldn't do his sums?

If the Mulroney campaign, by midsummer, could be described as over-slick, obviously the Turner campaign was distinctly unslick. Equally obviously, it was coming unstuck. Visibly, audibly, physically unstuck, held together by sticky tape and what used to pass for baling wire, except that baling wire used to work.

Inside the Turner camp, there was chaos, and argument, and bad blood, and lost tempers—all the things that once were thought of as Tory prerogatives. After all, it was the Conservatives who invented the game of "Swallow the Leader," devouring in turn John Bracken, George Drew, John Diefenbaker, Robert Stanfield, and Joe Clark. Was it possible that the Liberals, the party of prolonged leadership, would treat John Turner like a Tory?

From the vantage point of the Turner campaign bus or the chartered jet—indeed, anywhere within earshot of Turner and his advisers—you could tell something was wrong. Something, that is, beyond what the news reports and the polls were conveying, which was bad enough.

What was happening was that the Liberals' own private polls were foreshadowing what the published polls would reveal soon enough—the bottom was dropping out of the Turner campaign. The popular bulge from the leadership convention had dissolved, and things were in a state of free fall, with Turner conveying a confused image to the public instead of the resolute opening portrayal of the Chief Executive Officer. Even lifetime Liberals were being chased away by Turner's indecision and his espousal of what were regarded as Conservative fiscal and economic heresies. There were echoes of John Roberts' warning during the leadership campaign—if the voters are offered a choice between an imitation Conservative and a real one, they'll take the real one every time.

John Turner uses a traditional campaign technique of holding a baby while visiting delegates at a farm in Nova Scotia. (UPC/Michael Creagen)

John Turner flanked by senior policy advisor Shirley Seward (L) and Consumer and Corporate Affairs Minister Judy Erola (R) two days before leaders' debate on women's issues. (UPC/Ron Poling)

Prime Minister John Turner and Brian Mulroney "face" each other before the debate on women's issues. (UPC/Ryan Remiorz)

Conservative leader Brian Mulroney shakes hands with everyone but the dog while making his way through a crowd in Campbell River, B.C. (UPC/Mike Blake)

Brian Mulroney and his wife Mila show the "thumbs-up" sign in front of a large noon-time crowd in downtown Montreal. (UPC/Hans Deryk)

Lucille (L) and Ed Broadbent leave a studio with radio personality Betty Kennedy. (UPC/Ryan Remiorz)

NDP leader Ed Broadbent tries on a cowboy hat at a local rodeo event while on a campaign stop in Thunder Bay, Ontario. (UPC/Ryan Remiorz)

Former Prime Minister Joe Clark takes over as chef at a PC barbecue in Drayton Valley, Alberta. (UPC/Charles Palmer)

Brian Mulroney breakfasts with Robert Stanfield (back row right) and the four Atlantic provincial premiers. (UPC/Hans Deryk)

Jean Chrétien speaks with a group of Conservative supporters in Montreal. (UPC/Ryan Remiorz)

John Turner uses a pair of binoculars as he and Quebec Premier Réne Levèsque watch the trans-Atlantic sail boat races in Quebec City. (UPC/ Ron Poling)

John Turner talks with Ontario Liberal leader David Peterson. (UPC/ Andy Clark)

Brian Mulroney jokes with Ontario Premier Bill Davis. (UPC/Hans Deryk)

18

THAT SINKING FEELING

We were pondering these portents late on Tuesday, July 31, when a messenger brought in a press release, reading:

"I am pleased to announce that Senator Keith Davey has been offered and has accepted the position of national campaign co-chairperson. Signed, Bill Lee, National Campaign Director, Liberal Party of Canada."

These tidings were so patently ridiculous that I sent the document back, cursing people who play practical jokes when serious business was afoot.

But colleagues flocked around to assure me the handout was genuine, and there it was, coming in on the news service wires, making Turner a laughing stock and sending Conservatives and New Democrats into convulsions of delight.

The announcement called Turner's judgement into question on two counts, one being his initial selection of Lee as National Campaign Director, and the other being the summons to Davey.

Both Lee and Davey had reputations as heavy hitters in the game of political moving and shaking, and both reputations were vastly overblown. Lee had used his credentials to amass a fortune in the related trades of consulting and lobbying, while Davey had parlayed his own image into a position of power in the court of Pierre Trudeau.

Both had contributed to as many failures as successes in their traipse through the corridors of power. Lee had a large hand in the unification of the armed forces by his boss, Paul Hellyer, and he subsequently acted as adviser to Hellyer in the abortive bids for the Liberal leadership in 1968 and the Conservative leadership in 1978. Pierre Trudeau had taken him along in the Trudeaumania campaign of 1968, when the only advice Trudeau needed was to avoid being trampled or raped by his adoring fans.

John Turner had summoned Lee to rescue his leadership bid following Trudeau's retirement, when the initial momentum threatened to flag and Jean Chrétien was starting to come on.

Turner's victory was widely attributed to Lee, and you could see him in all the victory photographs, at Turner's side, sharing the moment of triumph.

Turner had called Lee back for the election campaign when he realized that Trudeau had let all the Grit election machinery fall into disuse, and that Turner's own team of amateurs didn't know how to play the election game. Back came Lee, and the word went out that everything had to be cleared with Bill, and that the campaign was in the very best of hands.

Maybe Lee's were the best hands available in the circumstances, but it was soon obvious that they couldn't run things the way Mulroney's people could. And even if they could, it was too late—Turner, by calling an early election, had caught himself with his own pants down.

There was no way Lee could be pleased to announce the appointment of Keith Davey. We could have believed him if he had said he was horrified to announce, or ashamed to announce, or even drunk to announce. But not pleased.

Davey was Trudeau's principal adviser, and Turner had been trying, ever since he won the leadership, to put distance between himself and Trudeau. Davey was a backroom manipulator against whom the youth wing of the party, with nods of approval from Turner, had rebelled two years previously. Davey was known as the rainmaker, and Turner had said there would be no rainmakers around his government.

Already there was one Liberal campaigner, Jean Chrétien, going around saying he was a better leader than Turner. Keith Davey was on record, earlier in the year, as saying Pierre Trudeau was a better man than Turner, or anybody else.

Davey had fought desperately to persuade Trudeau to stay on and fight a sixth campaign. This was one of the few matters on which Trudeau, after long months of wavering, rejected Davey's advice. Davey was the principal host at "The Last Supper," the big Toronto bash in Trudeau's honour. He was the man who planned and delivered the lavish tribute to Trudeau at the Liberal convention.

He was the man most consulted by Trudeau on patronage appointments, which is how Trudeau often bestowed rewards on party workers he had never seen, whose names he had never heard.

Beyond doubt, he had been consulted by Trudeau on the final patronage list that was unloaded on Turner with such devastating results. And he would have urged Trudeau to get a commitment in writing from Turner, remembering what happened when Trudeau himself took over from Lester Pearson in 1968. Davey was head of the Pearson team then, and there were appointments Pearson asked Trudeau to make, but Trudeau swept Pearson aside together with all his advisers and recommendations, and acted as though Pearson had never existed, until he dredged up his memory to help the 1983 peace initiative.

Could Davey work for Turner, and bring solutions to problems he himself had done so much to create?

Yes, he could. He could at least try.

Could Bill Lee and Keith Davey work together?

Behind the Liberal scenes the battle raged, with Lee insisting that he know where the money was coming from and where it was going, and demanding control of the pork-barrel advertising contracts, and coming up empty.

Turner, having been acclaimed as the Liberal candidate

in Vancouver Quadra, had a final meeting with his friend and benefactor at which Lee demanded carte blanche, and was told no.

At this point, according to Lee, he resigned.

According to Turner, Lee was fired.

Turner had decided to go the rest of the way with Davey, just as Trudeau had done after his near-defeat in 1972, when he called Davey back from exile and decided to get physical, and political, and dirty. What worked with Davey in 1972 might work again in 1984, except that there was so little time, and what time there was, was so short.

Davey threw the image of Gentleman John Turner out the window, and swung the tone of Turner's speeches to the left, and into the rough. No more Mr. Nice Guy, and Mulroney henceforth would be called a crook, a charlatan, and a liar.

The day before the Turner-Lee showdown, a poll commissioned by the CTV network, and conducted immediately after the TV debates, showed the Conservatives pulling ahead of the Liberals, a gap that would continue to widen in every subsequent poll until election day. September 4, John Turner kept insisting, was the only poll that would count, when the people cast their ballots. From his own private polls, he was beginning to realize that the official poll on election day might be the most devastating of all, the worst defeat in history, making Joe Clark look like a long-term prime minister, and making Turner the only prime minister who had held office without facing the House of Commons.

All through the month of August, the public opinion polls were like drumbeats of doom for the Liberals.

They were getting the same messages from their own private surveys, and these were causing anguish and strife inside the chaotic campaign apparatus.

But the published polls were knocking the props out from under Turner's campaign, demoralizing Liberal workers, speeding up the Conservative bandwagon, and generating a matching switch to the Tories in Quebec.

Arguments raged about the validity of public opinion polls at election time, and whether or not they actually influence the thinking of voters. On one thing there could be no argument—they influence the tone of reporting on a campaign, and they have a profound influence on commentators and columnists and editorial writers.

I have always said, about our trade, that we do not tell people what to think, but we try to tell them what to think about, and I believe that to be a fair assessment of the journalists' role. But the public opinion polls are now part of journalism, and they don't fit my precept, because they take a measurement of public opinion at a given point and, by publishing it, create a rash of headlines and newscasts that no mere journalist could generate. Our opinions and impressions have long helped to illuminate the political process, but they haven't influenced it the way the polls have.

The budgets of our major news gathering agencies were severely pinched in 1984, and election coverage expenses were the highest ever. Significant parts of the budgets of Southam News, the *Toronto Globe and Mail*, the *Toronto Star*, *La Presse*, CTV, and CBC were diverted into polling.

The resultant polls achieved more notoriety for their sponsors than could ever be obtained through mere news gathering, to the point where competition inside the media degenerated into a race to see who could produce the most polls.

In my own case, there was a cutback in the money available for election coverage, so the pace of polling could be stepped up and, as a result, the Southam name was emblazoned across the country as it had never been before. The tidings in those August polls were so grim for the Grits that Mrs. Geills Turner was moved to attack Southams as an anti-Liberal outfit, bringing a reply from our general manager, Nick Hills, that Mrs. Turner was a sore loser.

This involvement of our management in the actual campaign debate was nothing new. In 1963, John Diefenbaker had ordered Southam man Charles King off his campaign plane because King had written that "the Diefenbubble was bursting.'' We instructed King to stay with Dief to the end, and there were demonstrations at various airports across the country in King's support, with placards reading ''Charles King for Prime Minister.''

Our man Bruce Phillips was engaged in open dispute with Lester Pearson in 1963 and John Diefenbaker in 1965, and these contretemps certainly enlivened coverage of those campaigns, but they stemmed from the practice of our trade by gifted professionals. We comforted ourselves that our only sin was committing journalism.

In 1984, the commissioning and publishing of polls became a major aspect of political journalism, as practised not only by newspapers and news agencies, but by the great publicly owned broadcasting networks of the Canadian Broadcasting Corporation.

What was new about that was that the heirarchy of the CBC, unlike those of the privately owned news organizations, had an obvious stake in the election of a new Parliament, since that heirarchy is appointed by the elected government, and the CBC's operating budget consists largely of taxpayers' money voted by the elected members of the House of Commons. Corporation executives are accountable to Parliament and appear routinely before Commons committees.

Should a Crown corporation sponsor a poll to determine the political feelings of the electorate, and then turn the whole of its resources into publicising that poll, and analysing it, and concluding from it what the election results were going to be?

The answer, in the 1984 campaign, was a resounding yes, thus setting the pattern for all elections to come, for better or worse.

During the July portion of the 1984 campaign, the tone of coverage was set by a Gallup Poll taken between July 5 and July 7, just after John Turner called the election.

It showed the Liberals with 48 per cent of decided voters, the Conservatives with 39 percent, and the New Democrats with 11. The undecided segment was 39 per cent.

The first poll to come out in August was commissioned by the CTV network, and conducted by the Toronto polling firm Thompson, Lightstone, and it sent shock waves across the country with its message of Conservatives 45, Liberals 36, and New Democrats 17, with the undecideds at 33.

Brian Mulroney commented that the numbers were moving the right way, and Ed Broadbent said "by God, we're making gains," and Turner press aide Brian Smith said the only poll that counted was the one on election day.

From that point on, the successive polls received more coverage than the election campaign itself, and whatever debate there might have been about issues was lost in the welter of reports that the election was over and that a massive victory was coming for Mulroney, and a total defeat for Turner. Turner was in for the longest month in the life of any political loser, a month in the course of which media reports on polls would subject him to Canada's version of the torture of the thousand knives.

The poll that settled matters, or at least indicated that matters were going to be settled, was the Southam poll published on August 11, conducted by the Carleton School of Journalism polling unit. A July Southam poll had shown Liberals 45 per cent, Conservatives 42.5, and NDP 10.5. This one showed Conservative 51, Liberals 32, New Democrats 15.5, with 31 per cent undecided.

The poll had a smashing impact, not only in the Southam papers but everywhere—in print, on TV, on radio, on the campaign planes, and in every discussion and analysis of how the campaign was going.

The Southam poll, which in July had shown Turner 37 and Mulroney 22 on the question of prime ministerial competence, now showed Mulroney 29, Turner 26.

Southam coverage of the poll said it was a dramatic surge for the Tories, and quoted Carleton pollster Alan Frizzell as saying the results were evidence of Turner's early campaign blunders and his poor performance in the television debates, undermining voter confidence in his leadership abilities.

The most startling thing about the Southam poll was its measurement of voter thinking in Quebec. In July it had been Liberals 61, Conservatives 28, NDP 4. In August, it was Conservatives 49, Liberals 37, NDP 9.

The Southam poll dominated all campaign coverage until it was matched by the poll commissioned by the CBC, billed as the most complete and extensive survey of public opinion ever undertaken in Canadian politics. The CBC figures, conveyed in a special telecast as elaborate as the network's subsequent coverage of election night itself, told Canadians that a Tory landslide was taking place, and that the Liberals were doomed. The bandwagon was hitting on all cylinders, with all media horns blaring, and the election post-mortems started, three weeks before election day, with the accent on the make-up of Mulroney's cabinet, and the date of the future Liberal leadership convention.

19

ALL SCREWED UP

John Turner came up with a billion-dollar youth training program, a segment of which was dubbed "First Chance." It didn't catch on, and most Canadians seemed to think it was a new Pay TV network.

In Prince Rupert, B.C., reporters were clamouring for comment from Turner about the appointment of Senator Keith Davey, and they cornered him in the wheelhouse of a ferryboat, where he tried vainly to wait them out and was pictured peering furtively out the wheelhouse window.

Turner pleaded with reporters to "just write what we're saying."

Geills Turner complained there were more photos appearing of Mila Mulroney than of her.

Turner said that in British Columbia "the men are as great as the mountains," and Iona Campagnolo countered that "we also have women who are as great as the mountains."

Twelve million dollars' worth of television and radio commercials were unleashed on Canadian listeners and viewers, but the impact wasn't a fraction of that registered by the opinion polls.

In Baie Comeau, the first signs appeared that Brian Mulroney would win the riding of Manicouagan, and he promised that when he was in power, he would hold frequent cabinet meetings there.

From the campaign sidelines, the exiled Bill Lee said he had found himself increasingly distanced from Turner, trying to run an election apparatus which did not even exist, with Liberal headquarters in an antiquated barn, and no work done on campaign readiness for more than a year. The party had been let down, he said, by a planning committee of which the chairmen were Marc Lalonde and Keith Davey. Lee spared mention of Liberal President Iona Campagnolo, who had declined to run for the Liberal leadership on the grounds that she was too busy preparing the party for an election.

Lee criticized Turner's principal secretary, John Swift, for faulty briefings of the leader, adding: "All these months I've been working for no pay, no fee, and so have a good many other volunteers—unlike some highly paid people in other places who've just been messing up."

Lee was the source of some other colourful quotes, including one about how Jean Chrétien had complained to him in the July campaigning that Lalonde was making him a laughing stock in Quebec. Lee telephoned Lalonde to ask him to play ball with Chrétien, and Lalonde's reply was "screw him."

And from Lee came the story of how Marc Lalonde really did want to run for re-election, on the assurance that he would continue to be Turner's finance minister. When Lalonde phoned for an answer, interrupting a Turner strategy session at 24 Sussex Drive, Turner's reaction was "oh, shit." He told Lalonde no.

Lee's account of his final meeting with Turner at the prime minister's Harrington Lake retreat had Turner asking him: "Bill, tell me honestly. Do you think I've sold out to the party establishment?"

To which Lee says he replied: "Yes John, I do. I'm sorry."

The *Toronto Star* quoted Lee as saying that Turner, looking like a "wounded, cornered animal," sat in his deep chair, squinting his eyes, murmuring over and over, "I've screwed up. I've screwed it all up, I don't know what to do."

Keep in mind that Lee is a businessman who sells his services to the highest bidder and that he, like Liberal pollster Martin Goldfarb, sought to keep his head when all about him were losing theirs. The need to preserve "the product" was illustrated in Lee's account of an exchange with Goldfarb, in which the pollster complained of the party's use of Winnipeg pollster Angus Reid, whose surveys were more negative than Goldfarb's.

Lee gave this account to Linda Diebel of the *Montreal Gazette*:

"Bill," said Goldfarb, "you can't do this to me. I've got big U.S. clients who rely on the fact that I advise the prime minister."

To which Lee replied: "Jesus, Marty, I don't believe this. I know that you've got both (Senator Michael) Kirby and (Tom) Axworthy on your payroll."

"Well, you're right," Goldfarb replied, "but they are both very able individuals. I plan to continue to use their services."

Back in Sept-Isles, Brian Mulroney made his first prediction of a solid Tory breakthrough in Quebec, and he and Mila boogied the night away in a Sept-Isles' disco.

Reporters' noses twitched when the tabloid *Montreal Sunday Express* reported that Mulroney had been a director of a company whose subsidiary distributed pornographic video tapes. The company turned out to be media giant Standard Broadcasting, and the subsidiary was CTA Video distributors Ltd.

CTA financial manager David Kennedy delivered one of the great quotes of the campaign when he said the tapes cited by the newspaper, titled Bizarre Sex Devices and Rape of Love, were edited versions of hard-core porn, "and it's much the same as watching a football game with all the touchdowns deleted."

Mulroney said all CTA video tapes had been screened and edited by the Ontario Censor Board, and the matter ended there.

The mayor of Schefferville, the town that Mulroney had shut down in 1982 when he was president of the Iron Ore Company, announced he was voting Tory. Mayor Yvan Belanger said Mulroney represented the only hope of putting the town on its feet.

Mulroney's Liberal opponent in Manicouagan, incumbent André Maltais, said he didn't want John Turner in the riding because "the fight is between two guys from the North Shore and Turner wouldn't relate well."

Mulroney made his first direct appeal to Quebeckers who voted Yes in the 1980 independence referendum, telling his nomination meeting in Sept-Isles: "The men and women of Quebec love Quebec and are proud of Canada. But they also love Canada and are proud of Quebec. Their hearts are big enough for both these allegiances. Very few of those who said Yes to Quebec said No to Canada, and no one who said Yes to Canada said No to Quebec."

In Prince Edward Island, reporters clamoured for access to John Turner, and he replied: "Just watch what we're doing. Just listen to me and watch me. Watch this afternoon and this evening."

When nothing emerged, a Turner aide snapped: "What do you expect? Every time we open our mouths, it's distorted."

Turner accused Mulroney of recruiting three separatists to run as Progressive Conservative candidates in Quebec—Suzanne Duplessis in Louis-Hébert, Pierre Ménard in Hull, and Monique Vézina in Rimouski.

Duplessis and Vézina said they had worked for the Yes campaign in the referendum, and Ménard said he had given up his membership in the Parti Québécois.

This opening of old wounds kicked back on Turner with Quebec voters, as would become clear on election night when they turned away from their Liberal past and embraced the Mulroney approach to the future. Duplessis and Vézina won decisive victories, and Ménard missed upsetting old Liberal warhorse Gaston Isabelle by a mere 1,000 votes.

In Ontario, Mulroney was campaigning with Premier

William Davis at his side—that same Davis who had said "no" to Mulroney's plea that he declare Ontario a bilingual province.

That matter was not mentioned as the two men surged through Western Ontario, laying waste Liberal strongholds along the way.

In Windsor, Mulroney said he hadn't seen John Turner around when he himself was in the trenches fighting for Canada during the 1980 Quebec referendum. He said: "Canada has had enough of the combat zone of Liberal bitterness and personal antipathy that dominated federal-provincial relations too long. This is the time to bring people together. This is the time to heal old wounds, not to settle old scores."

That line would recur in every Mulroney speech to the end of the campaign, along with the Turner quote on patronage, "the devil made me do it."

And when opponents and editorialists insisted that Mulroney reconcile his open-handed attitude to the Quebec government with his 1983 rejection of René Lévesque and all his works, Mulroney went into a buttoned-up configuration that continued to September 4. He knew he had struck a chord with Quebeckers, and he was content to let it reverberate to an election night crescendo.

In Vancouver, facing personal defeat in the riding of North Vancouver-Burnaby, Iona Campagnolo, saying that someone had to take the initiative, called for a mutual, verifiable nuclear arms freeze. And in Winnipeg, Jean Chrétien said he personally advocated NATO's renouncing the first use of nuclear weapons.

Turner, sore beset, said he intended to fulfil Canada's commitments to her allies, adding, in reference to Campagnolo, that "I welcome her original comments and will try to reconcile them with the objectives of our allies around the world."

Meanwhile, the Liberal leader was subjected to a rash of headlines about his pants.

The scene was the Martinet restaurant, in Trois Rivières, where Turner was having dinner with local dignitaries, hosted by the Quebec hatchetman of the Liberal cabinet, Privy Council President André Ouellet.

In the midst of the festivities, a waiter dumped coffee on Turner's lap, staining his grey flannels.

Ouellet led Turner to a nearby washroom, trying to avoid campaign reporters who were gathered at the bar. Turner and Ouellet disappeared into the washroom and, in a few moments, Ouellet emerged, carrying Turner's trousers.

Ouellet walked down the hall and sidestepped into the women's washroom with Mrs. Geills Turner, who set to work to clean the stain from the PM's flannels, which were duly returned to Turner by Ouellet, back in the men's room.

A photographer and a technician who were in the men's can when Turner and Ouellet entered, reported that Turner had peeled off his pants saying: ''Take them down to Geills, and she'll take care of them.''

She did, indeed. And the resulting national debate almost equalled in intensity the earlier bruhaha about Turner's bum patting tendencies. Was it demeaning to expect the wife to clean the pants? Couldn't Turner clean his own?

Truly, Murphy's Law was working overtime against Turner, and the incident cost him with men and women alike. Worse, it made him a laughing stock, and if there is anything a political leader is not supposed to be in an election, it is that. You could check it with Joe Clark.

Turner's press aide on the campaign, former CBC broadcaster Dennis Baxter, was grounded and replaced by Pierre Trudeau's one-time press aide, Lieutenant-Colonel Ralph Coleman, on leave of absence from the armed forces. Coleman barely got himself unlimbered when it was pointed out that his activity was in violation of Canadian Armed Forces regulations, so he disappeared, replaced by former Trudeau press secretary Brian Smith, who had worked against Turner and for Jean Chrétien in the leadership campaign.

In Quebec, Premier Réne Lévesque predicted Conservative gains in his province, praising Mulroney for promising better federal-provincial cooperation. Lévesque welcomed what he called "the abandonment of forced centralization which has been in charge in Ottawa for twenty years." He wasn't endorsing the Tories, but he said members of his Parti Québécois were working for all federal parties except the federal Liberals. And since they weren't working for the separatist Parti Nationaliste— "though they're free to," grinned Lévesque—that left only the Tories.

And in all Quebec media, the tone of reporting swung to the Conservative side, with editorial endorsements from Mulroney piling up, and the popular Montreal tabloid *Journal de Montreal* carrying headlines about a potential mania for the Tory leader. No previous federal election had ever received such intensive coverage in the French-language press, radio, and TV.

By now, it seemed that Mulroney could do no wrong.

His predecessor, Joe Clark, had angered the Arabs with his promise to move the Canadian embassy in Israel from Tel Aviv to Jerusalem. When the Arab nations lowered the boom on Clark, the promise was shelved, and Canadians poured scorn not on the Arabs, but on Clark.

Mulroney got Arab dander up by lumping Israel together with the U.S., Britain, and France as one of Canada's traditional friends, and denouncing the appearance of a representative of the Palestine Liberation Organization before the Senate committee on foreign affairs during the last parliamentary session.

If he had been prime minister, he said, he would not have allowed the appearance by Zehdi Terzi, the United Nations representative of the PLO, and he promised there would be no such hearings in future, if he gained power.

The Council of Arab Ambassadors in Ottawa issued a statement deploring "this new definition of Canadian foreign policy, which ruptures the traditional base of Canada's equilibrium in its relations with all countries of the Middle East."

Abdullah Abdullah, director of the Palestine Information Office in Ottawa, warned that the cultural, economic, and political ties between Canada and the Arab world would be affected if Mulroney denied the Palestinians' right to self-determination.

The incident scarcely rippled the election waters, and what backwash there was seemed to flow more against the Arab spokesmen than against Mulroney.

Joe Clark might have pondered the injustice of it all, but he didn't let it show. Instead, he spent the closing weeks of the campaign stumping for the Mulroney team—in Quebec, and across the Prairies, where he pledged to "leave no stone unturned, no socialist unturfed." Clark praised Mulroney at every opportunity, and Tory Saskatchewan strongman Ray Hnatyshyn told him "you are a person whose reputation is being enhanced every day you perform in public life."

Obviously, Clark was preaching for a call. Equally obviously, though, he was demonstrating the real miracle of Mulroney, helped by the prospect of power. The Conservative Party was sticking together.

Perhaps, as some suggested, it was "wimpy" of Clark to strive so hard for the man who had whipped him out of his leadership. It might have been better for him to have withdrawn to Olympian heights, as Trudeau did. But it was worth remembering that Clark was twenty years younger than Trudeau, with a lot of political ambition to fulfil. And besides, Clark didn't have $20 million to call his own. What he had was his pay as an MP and a few thousand bucks profit on the Ottawa house that he and Maureen McTeer had bought in 1983, and decided they didn't like. They bought a new abode from Rusins Kaufmanis, the *Ottawa Citizen* cartoonist whose drawings had savaged Clark throughout his years of leadership.

20

UP WITH WOMEN!

The final television debate of the campaign took place in Toronto on the evening of August 15, and it was supposed to be by, for, and about women and the issues that concern them most.

It became known as Ed Broadbent Night in Canada, tailor-made for the New Democrats who have had the militant feminist movement locked up since its emergence as a political and social factor in Canadian life.

How much a political and social factor it is, in political terms, remains questionable. Ed Broadbent won the TV debate without raising a sweat, and the most that could be said for John Turner and Brian Mulroney was that they avoided the verbal custard pies thrown at them, and stopped short of declaring Canada a matriarchy now and forevermore.

The intended accent on women received a bit of a setback when Mulroney chose the occasion to say that, by August 28, he would reveal the costs of his party's campaign promises.

This stole a lot of the attention and gave the Liberals something to talk about for the ensuing thirteen days and nights, even though they knew, as just about everybody did, that Mulroney was stalling and had no intention of itemizing his accounts in public. Besides, there had never been a Canadian election in which campaigners put price tags on their promises, and it was unlikely that Mulroney was going to set a precedent now.

As television, the debate was a throwback to the Major Bowes Amateur Hour, and the opening segment, in French, was calculated to send English-speaking viewers straight to bed.

The big hit of the night, if there was one, was panelist Kay Sigurjonsson, once a familiar CBC presenter, who brought cheers with her question: "Why should we trust you now?"

Just what was so historic about that query was not totally clear, since voters had been asking that of politicians ever since ancient Greece, without ever receiving a convincing reply.

It has long been considered the one unanswerable question in politics, the only reposte being something like "would you rather live in Chile? Or El Salvador? Or Lebanon? Russia, anyone?"

Years ago, Winston Churchill gained attention with his statement that parliamentary democracy was the worst system in the world, except for all the others. The attempted isolation of women's issues in the August 15th TV debate may have been a moment in history, as its promoters insisted, certified as such by Chaviva Hosek, president of the National Action Committee on the Status of Women, who conned the networks into carrying it.

She said she had never seen political leaders so well briefed on women's issues, and she reminded us that women constitute 52 per cent of the electorate.

What the debate showed, though, if it showed anything, was that women's interests are not confined to women's issues, and that they extend to every issue in society, with emphasis on the economic.

There was a lot of weaving and dodging on the issue of equal pay for work of equal value, with Broadbent sounding the most convinced and most convincing, causing Turner to say, amid boos and hisses, that everybody knew Broadbent would never come to power anyway.

Here is an account of my own adventures on the night of the women's debate, when I gained access to the halls of Ottawa's Algonquin College, where four hundred women had gathered to view the proceedings on big TV screens, with the promise of extended discussion afterwards.

There I was, sitting in a roomful of women waiting for their issues to be ventilated.

No sooner did the program from Toronto get under way than the CBC crew in the room turned on the bright lights to shoot audience reaction, and the picture on the big screen was blotted out.

I let out a howl of protest, but found myself a lonely voice. No womanly cries joined mine in demanding the bright lights be doused.

"Come on, women!" I roared. "We came here to see a show, not be one!"

The woman in front of me told me to pipe down, that this was a CBC television crew shooting, and if I didn't like it, I could leave. She wanted to hear no more haranguing from me.

Cowed, I subsided, and when the TV guys had finished shooting, the picture on the giant screen became visible again and I settled down, with the women, to follow the "debate."

What it turned into was a town meeting of the New Democratic Party, much, it seemed, like the roomful of Toronto women in which the show was being shot. So far as the live audience was concerned, it was Broadbent's night, and while I am a fan of the NDP leader, I doubt he is as great a debater as those women thought he was.

I tried to catch the spirit of the affair but couldn't bring myself to hiss, or laugh, every time John Turner or Brian Mulroney tried to dance to the tune of the questioners, all of whom seemed as popular with the audience as Broadbent himself.

One of our problems in the Ottawa hall was that the sound system was set up by men, and it was lousy. There is no reason why women could not set up their own sound system, since most of the components are assembled by women in far-off Japan, Taiwan, or Korea, but I have yet to encounter a sound system run by women.

This particular male-oriented system either gave us too much French and too little English, or equal mounts of both, or no audible sound at all, so we were left with the spectacle of Broadbent, Turner, and Mulroney gumming one another, and their questioners making fierce faces, asking if they had stopped beating their wives, while women kept talking at the back of the hall, or leaving to go home and watch the debate on their own TVs.

Broadbent's voice came through more loudly than the others, and when he advocated that there be a quota on bank loans for women, there were cheers from the crowd. He got another ovation for freedom of choice on abortion, saying no woman should be forced to have one, and John Turner drew groans when he advocated that present abortion laws be applied equally across the land.

There was applause when Broadbent advocated an immediate nuclear freeze, but when Mulroney said he had supported Pierre Trudeau's peace initiative, a woman's voice in the audience said, ''blah, blah, blah!'' and the place broke up.

The suggestion that the needs of beaten women be put ahead of the requirements of the armed forces was cheered, and when Mulroney said he would match provincial expenditures on rape crisis centres, a woman shouted ''fucking nerve!''

Broadbent's chiding of Turner and Mulroney for vagueness was roundly applauded, and there was much thigh-slapping when Turner said ''we must get at pornography.''

Broadbent said child care centres were as much a basic right as medicare, and when Turner frowned, there was merriment in the hall.

Broadbent attacked benefits that go to ''fairly wealthy women'' (cheers), and Mulroney said there would be no cuts in benefits ''for those in need'' (groans). Turner said there would be no cuts, period, and got his first handclaps of the night.

Mulroney said he couldn't say why women voters

should trust him now, but added: "I am as committed to this as we all are."

There followed a post-mortem on the debate by local resource women, plus comments from the audience and a bearpit session with female representatives of the political parties, including the woman who had got me into the hall in the first place, my co-vivant, Ms. Claudy Mailly, who was trying to overcome a 30,000 Liberal majority and win the Quebec riding of Gatineau for the Conservatives. (She did, too, winning by over 8,000 votes, thus qualifying me for the Parliamentary Spouses Association. But that is next year's book.)

Most of the post-debate discussion was inaudible because of the wretched sound system.

At the end, everybody filled in scorecards that showed Broadbent the winner, with 87 per cent.

In line with my well-known impartiality and detachment from events, I didn't fill in my card, but if I had, it would have been a 50-50 tie between Turner and Mulroney for merely showing up, and zero for the sound men and the male camera crews.

I doubt that the debate swayed a single vote, male or female, and bum patting wasn't mentioned once, which was just as well.

21

THE FALL

On August 17, the *Toronto Star* announced publication of the first biography of John Turner, by my old Australian cobber, Jack Cahill, who had taken four months off to write the life story of Canada's 17th prime minister.

"A rare insight into the real John Turner, past and present," trumpeted the *Star*, noting that the book was subtitled "The Long Run."

Cahill had been granted twenty hours of interviews by Turner, which would turn out to be a sizeable slice out of his total time as prime minister.

Brian Mulroney, back on tour, turned a deaf ear to reporters' questions and, when a man in Laval asked if he favoured capital punishment, his reply was recorded as "ah-ha-ha-ha."

In Niagara Falls, Liberal incumbent Arthur MacBain was ordered by a human rights tribunal to pay $1,500 to a former employee who accused him of sexually harassing her.

MacBain said he would go public with his side of the case "regardless of who it hurts." He did, and the one it hurt was himself. On election day, he lost by a margin of almost three to one.

In Toronto, Conservative Energy Critic Pat Carney spoke to two hundred business executives and said it was one of her few chances to talk on energy policy in the campaign "because the producing provinces and the big consuming provinces and the premiers and energy ministers have a quiet little accord going that we did not want energy to be an issue, for the reason that energy policy has been a source of great bitterness in the country."

The Liberals took up Carney's words and trumpeted them across the land, but the issue didn't catch on, even when the New Democrats hammered away at it as a sellout to the multinationals. Carney protested that her words had been misinterpreted by media.

In Montreal, John Turner's campaign "star," Raymond Garneau, who quit as president of the City and District Savings Bank to run, said Canadians should look beyond Turner's perceived campaign errors to consider the benefits received from a federal Liberal government. He said Turner's main problem was that he was too much of a gentleman and a statesman.

Quebeckers would not agree on election day, though Garneau would gain a narrow, 2,000-vote win in the riding of Laval-des-Rapides, once the domain of Governor General Jeanne Sauvé, who won it by 29,000 votes in 1980.

In Valleyfield, Mulroney firmed up his promise of a new approach to Ottawa-Quebec relations, saying brutal and foolish quarrels must end, and adding: "We don't perceive the government of Quebec as an enemy. We see them as a government with whom we can work loyally to create jobs."

In Winnipeg, Turner said he had written to Soviet President Konstantin Chernenko asking for a meeting to discuss an international pact on arms control and disarmament. It was a follow-up to Turner's letter to U.N. Secretary-General Javier Peres de Cuellar, proposing a meeting of the major nuclear powers to discuss limiting nuclear stockpiles.

Chernenko's reply to Turner resembled the reaction of the Portuguese government to the nomination of Bryce Mackasey as Canadian ambassador. Nothing. Not even a "nyet." In fact, between the time of Turner's letter and election day, nobody could find Chernenko, and there was a suggestion he might be hiding to avoid involvement in the Canadian election. Just in case, Mulroney said in Gander, Newfoundland, that he supported Turner's letter to Chernenko, saying "peace is a major part of our program and I speak of it constantly."

In Cornerbrook, Newfoundland, Mulroney said it was wrong of Turner to suggest a Tory government would introduce a means test for social programs. Universality, he said, was "a sacred trust."

On August 18, a Southam News poll of voters in the riding of Vancouver Quadra indicated 50 per cent Conservative, 27 per cent Liberal, and 21 per cent New Democrat, with 33 per cent of respondents saying their opinion of John Turner had gone down during the campaign.

The poll was described as accurate within 6 per cent, 19 times out of 20, according to the formula of the Carleton University polling unit. The impression that Turner was losing to incumbent Bill Clarke in Quadra would persist right up to election day, when Turner finished 4,000 votes ahead. A last-minute sympathy vote, wept the Tories.

In Oshawa on August 19, Turner said "I've got lots of faults, but I believe I have been honest and I believe I can be trusted."

That same day, in an interview with *La Presse*, the Liberal incumbent in the Quebec riding of Argenteuil-Papineau, Robert Gourd, suggested that Jean Chrétien would be the logical successor to John Turner if the Liberals lost the election.

"John Turner will have taken the Liberal Party a step backward," said Gourd. "The day after defeat we shall have to begin the job of rebuilding the Liberal Party of Canada, and it's certainly Jean Chrétien who will take over, and we will take four steps ahead instead of backing up."

Told of Gourd's remarks, Mulroney clapped his hands and said: "Gourd doesn't know it, but by nightfall he's going to be the most famous Liberal in Canada." And the Tory leader used the Gourd quotes for the rest of the campaign. On election day, Gourd lost to Lise Bourgault of the PCs by 9,000 votes.

In Charlottetown, the annual meeting of provincial premiers ended with a communiqué calling on whoever became prime minister on September 4 to hold an immediate federal-provincial conference on the economy. Between the lines was the message that all ten of the premiers were hoping for the defeat of the Liberal government, and that nine out of the ten were betting on Brian Mulroney—the seven Tory premiers, plus B.C.'s Bennett and Quebec's Lévesque. Headlined the *Toronto Star*: "Premiers Pant at Scent of Tory Win."

With two weeks to go in the campaign, word came from Liberal headquarters in Ottawa that party strategists wanted Pierre Trudeau to play a major role in the closing phase. Trudeau, if he got the message, didn't respond.

In Ottawa, the largest contract available in Canadian advertising, representing some $60 million a year, was signed between the Department of Supply and Services and Canadian Media Corporation. CMC is jointly owned by three advertising giants with close ties to the Liberal Party—Vickers & Benson Co. Ltd., Ronalds-Reynolds and Co. Ltd. of Toronto, and Publicité BCP Ltée of Montreal.

(Vickers & Benson and Ronalds-Reynolds, together with MacLaren Advertising, supply the employees to staff Red Leaf Communications, the umbrella organization that handles Liberal advertising during election campaigns, under master manipulator Senator Jerry Grafstein. Grafstein's fight with Bill Lee over accounting procedures, with Keith Davey backing Grafstein, was one of the reasons for Lee's abrupt departure as Liberal campaign director, and his replacement by Davey.)

An Ottawa news conference was called by the prime minister's office to announce a new type of indexed government bond, designed to save taxpayers $2.2 billion over a four-year period if enough bonds were sold and if inflation stayed below 10 per cent. The spokesmen explaining the plan didn't seem to understand it, and it fell into the campaign rhetoric with a dull thud.

In Simcoe, Ontario, Geills Turner said she supported a

nuclear freeze and believed her husband did, too, along with Liberal candidates Iona Campagnolo and Lloyd Axworthy. Every serious member of the human race must favour a freeze, said Mrs. Turner.

On August 22, Keith Davey said the results of the public opinion polls were destroying the morale of Liberal campaign workers. He kept insisting the polls were out of date, and that the Liberals' own polls showed a rebound, but added: "I don't argue for a moment that the polls are not debilitating. They certainly are. They are very morale destroying. They are very tough to take. I don't minimize that at all. I couldn't agree more. But the media are writing us off much too quickly, and predictions of a Tory majority will be proven wrong. It's been a downer, but I've informed our people that we have polls taken overnight which indicate that we're on a roll."

In Montreal, Liberal candidate Raymond Garneau said Pierre Trudeau should stay out of the campaign, so the emphasis could be "looking to the future." "Maybe in four or five years when things have settled down he may intervene," said Garneau, "but now I don't think it should be done." (Trudeau did appear briefly in Toronto Spadina and in several Montreal ridings, but his only comment on the campaign was that "Mr. Turner is doing very well." Turner said "I would hope that perhaps we could have a joint appearance." They didn't.)

In Ottawa, a memo from NDP campaign director Gerry Caplan acknowledged that the Tories were headed for a big majority, and urged NDP candidates to run as "the conscience of Parliament" to fight Tory claims that an NDP vote was a wasted vote.

Toronto Sun publisher J.D. Creighton wrote an editorial in which he said his paper would support Mulroney, but adding that "the manner in which the media has attacked John Turner consistently, since his ascendency to be prime minister, fills me with despair. It's time for cheap-shot journalism to stop. John Turner is an honourable, intelligent, decent man whose public service is a matter of record."

Creighton and Turner were fellow patrons and table-holders at Winstons when both were piling up their fortunes at their respective trades.

The same issue of the *Sun* that contained Creighton's outburst carried a story from Chatham, Ontario, about how Turner had abandoned the high road of campaigning and had gotten "down and dirty."

What happened was that under the guidance of Keith Davey, Turner's speeches and the tone of Liberal advertising homed in on Brian Mulroney, accusing him of being a welcher and a charlatan.

In Chatham, Turner asked: "Can Canadians believe Brian Mulroney's words about Liberal social programs being a sacred Tory trust?"

He added: "I say to Mr. Mulroney that liberalism must be in the heart." And when the crowd cheered, he glowed: "We've got the momentum now."

But in that same Chatham speech, Turner said something that was more valid and revealing about himself. He said: "I have tried to conduct a frank, direct campaign. I believe that, of all the qualities I have and I may not have, one I have is honesty. Maybe Mr. Mulroney thinks he has it all won. Maybe some of the media does, too. But I will tell you, the Canadian people are reserving their judgement until September 4."

From that point on, Turner would hint at his distaste for his personal attacks on Mulroney by mentioning his own shortcomings, and indicating that his were the tactics of desperation, forced on him by the prospect of massive defeat.

In London, Ontario, he interjected these words into his prepared text: "I'm as human and as fallible as anybody in this room and I have, oh yes, I have some faults, and I've made my mistakes, but there is one virtue, I think, that even my opponents recognize, I have been honest with the Canadian people throughout this election.

In Thunder Bay, it was: "I have said across the country, yes, I may have some weaknesses, and some faults, but I have been honest."

And in a radio interview on August 22: "I am not running my campaign. Senator Davey is running that campaign and we have campaign co-chairs right across the country. All I am asking from the media is that they report me fairly, that they play the election as fairly as they can. We both have a duty toward the Canadian people so that there is a knowledgeable electorate and the people understand what the government is trying to do, and I recognize that any politician will try to arrange the facts and, to a certain extent, manage the news. It is up to the media to try to pierce that."

ON THE JETS

With the polls and the campaign strategists providing so much of the news, the leaders' jets were not as important to media as they had been in previous elections, but nonetheless we bought the seats at prices up to $8,000 each and thus helped subsidize the charter costs for the political parties.

Both John Turner and Brian Mulroney, having been burned by publication of what they thought were off-the-record exchanges, stayed mute to their fellow travellers of press, radio, and TV, who were forced to get the most vital tidings off the news wires and the digests of news reports from elsewhere, usually the media hotspots of the nation, Toronto, Ottawa, and Montreal.

The Broadbent plane was the most pleasant for campaign travel, being the least crowded, and the NDP leader being the most expansive and uninhibited.

The Mulroney plane was the largest and most luxurious, a three-engined Boeing 727 aboard which every comfort for reporters was attended to, short of access to Mulroney himself.

Aboard Turner's twin-engined DC-9, conditions were cramped and, for the most part, tense. Turner was obliged to share the cabin with the men and women he came to regard as his media tormentors, whose tempers were shortened by the constant uncertainties about where the Turner entourage was flying, and why. The aggravation was reflected in the tone of the reporting.

I spent the ten days prior to Mulroney's "revelation of costs" speech alternating between the jets of Mulroney and Turner, and here are a couple of snapshots taken at first hand.

First, Mulroney in Calgary, on the evening of August 22.

The man had the look of eagles in his eyes, flying across the friendly West and drawing cheers with his vision of prosperity in far-off Newfoundland, in Quebec, in Ontario, and laying his French on them amid applause.

He topped it by pledging: "I shall not rest until Western Canada is brought back to the cabinet table." Prolonged cheers.

It was a political spectacle not seen in these parts since the mania days of Pierre Trudeau or John Diefenbaker, and even Premier Peter Lougheed, looking out at the huge crowd on the banks of Calgary's Bow River, said "wow!"

For Brian Mulroney, it was the climax of a dream day of campaigning in Saskatchewan and Alberta, a day in which the speaking came easy and the cheers were there for the asking.

The Calgary crowd would have cheered him just for reading the telephone book. In Saskatoon and Regina, he had to work harder, so he put the wood to the New Democrats with his line about how they were wedded to the Grits, forevermore.

This was my fifteenth Canadian election, and only in the company of Trudeau in 1968, and Diefenbaker ten years earlier, had I seen elation like this both in the candidate and the crowds.

He even throws in some western inflections—ya gotta believe it, lookit, I tell ya, there's nothin' wrong with Canada, we're gonna build a brand new land. And this was the man who could talk to Quebeckers that same way, with their own inflections, in their own language.

Lougheed called Mulroney "Mr. Prime Minister," and earlier, Premier Grant Devine of Saskatchewan had said all the provincial premiers were pulling for a Tory win, with even René Lévesque saying Mulroney would sweep Quebec. (What Lévesque really said was that there would be Tory gains in Quebec, which isn't quite the same thing considering the Tories started from a base of one seat, but Saskatchewaners cheered anyway.)

At the Regina meeting Mulroney had promised better drinking water for the city, and when I asked a local scribe what the problem was, they handed me a glass of the stuff and I took a swig.

My gagging at the press table very nearly stopped the meeting.

"What is this?" I croaked.

"Algae," came the answer. "Try to pretend it tastes like corn on the cob, if you eat it husk and all,"

I asked if the populace was hardened to the taste, and got the brusque answer that the local custom was to mix it with rye whisky.

"Water means more than jobs," said Mulroney, "it means good health." We took off for Calgary, coughing.

The big Calgary meeting was as memorable in its way as the outdoor meeting in Victoria that kicked off Trudeaumania in 1958. That time, Pierre Trudeau descended from the skies in a helicopter to the roars of 10,000 people, a scene that came to be described as the First Coming. In Calgary, the crowd estimate for Mulroney was the same, though it was hard to tell with enthusiasts scattered among the trees of Prince's Island park.

Mulroney and the ever-present, ever-precious Mila arrived in a fancy carriage drawn by two prancing horses, skittering at the sight of a towering hot-air balloon moored behind the platform.

Lougheed gave Mulroney a branding iron and told him to burn the letters PC into Parliament "and keep them there for just a heck of a long time."

Mulroney obliged with selections from his campaign jokebook at John Turner's expense, including acknowledgment of a lone heckler—"The Grits are running a lean campaign. They can only send one heckler and send him to the only place he can find a crowd." Hours before, he had used the same crack to skewer the NDP in Regina and Saskatoon.

Diefenbaker used to re-cycle his own campaign material by the hour, day, and week, and Mulroney follows on, evoking the Old Chief's name. What a young fella from Prince Albert did a quarter of a century ago, a young fella from Baie Comeau can repeat.

But Mulroney has a weapon John Diefenbaker lacked, his identity as a true lingo-jingo Quebecker, whose mother was an O'Shea. Here in the West, he uses his French more as a talisman than as a means of communication—the "hey, get a load of this" approach. And the words he uses in French get through to Anglo ears, hearing words that sound like Canadian—prosperity, cooperation, fraternity, and *l'amour, toujours, l'amour.*

Mulroney calls it the grand alliance, and whatever it is, Westerners seem to be ready for it.

From Calgary, we flew on to British Columbia, where Mulroney had set his sights on six seats won by the New Democrats in 1980. He ignored ridings that were thought to be safe for the Tory incumbents, including Vancouver Quadra, where Bill Clarke was fighting John Turner, and North Vancouver-Burnaby, where Chuck Cook was being challenged by Iona Campagnolo. Cook drubbed Campagnolo all right, but Turner nipped Clarke, who was left to wonder if a visit by Mulroney might have saved him, and whether Mulroney was wrong to brush off TV hotliner Jack Webster the way he did. "Nobody brushes off Webster," snorted Webster.

"We're going down the gunbarrel," said Mulroney, explaining his concentration on the New Democratic seats, and his judgement was vindicated on election day when the Tories won three of the six—Kootenay East-Revelstoke, Kootenay West, and Nanaimo-Alberni. The other three—Kamloops-Shuswap, Cowichan-Malahat-The Islands, and Comox-Powell River—stayed with the NDP.

Here is Mulroney on tour in British Columbia, with the hecklers in hot pursuit:

He pulled doughty old Howard Green out of the political woodwork to prove the Tories invented nuclear disarmament, and he put the peacenik demonstrators to rout.

Then he roused himself into a fiery passage in French to confound western separatist hecklers who were shouting "free the West" and "separate or surrender to the French."

On both occasions, his open-air Vancouver Island audiences cheered.

The crowds were big, from Campbell River down to the outskirts of Victoria, with Mulroney gunning for the three NDP seats on the island.

One of the NDP incumbents, Ray Skelly of Comox-Powell River, attended the Mulroney rallies and said he'd never had so much personal publicity in his life, because Mulroney mentioned his name so often.

The Tory leader identified every heckler as a Skelly supporter, even though the demonstrators were either nuclear freeze advocates or opposed to French.

And on his last day in British Columbia, he continued his argument that a vote for the NDP was a vote for the Liberals, even though that thesis could only apply to a minority Parliament, and the Tories were clearly headed for a majority.

Mulroney's final, and finest, moment was at the rally outside Victoria, on the site of what once was an anti-aircraft battery, when Doug Christie and his followers in the Western Canada Concept voiced their hatred of bilingualism.

Mulroney's custom has been to give western audiences small doses of his fluent French, keeping it simple and direct. Always, Westerners cheer him.

On this occasion, Mulroney clenched his fist at a sign reading "French fraud" and, in French, shouted words that could become as memorable as Pierre Trudeau's famous stand against the St. Jean Baptiste bottle-throwers in Montreal, on the eve of the 1968 election.

That action was reckoned to be worth 100,000 votes to Trudeau in English-speaking Canada. Mulroney's words might net him a similar number of votes in French Canada, because what he said in French to the hecklers was "I want to tell you that Canada, our dear Canada, we want unity, harmony, and prosperity for everyone."

And the Anglo crowd roared its approval—a crowd so Anglo that in his usual litany of Canada's best friends in the world, Mulroney for the first time put the United Kingdom ahead of the United States.

Mulroney's French-speaking advisers called it his finest moment of the campaign, though to admit that would be to give the handful of hecklers an importance they didn't deserve, because the cause of western separatism is in such tatters.

Mulroney's neatest trick of the trip was pulling Howard Green out of the hat on the nuclear issue.

He did it first in Campbell River when, confronted with a nuclear freeze petition, he recalled that more than twenty years ago it had been Green, as John Diefenbaker's foreign minister, who had campaigned for global disarmament.

And Green, Mulroney said, was a great British Columbian.

The crowd applauded, so at the next island stop, in Courtenay, Mulroney sharpened the reference, recalling that Green had fought with Diefenbaker to keep nuclear weapons out of Canada, only to lose the 1963 election at the hands of the combined Liberals and New Democrats, whereupon nuclear warheads came to Canadian soil.

There were loud cheers, and Mulroney might have been forgiven for wishing he had resurrected Green earlier (in fact, Green was alive and well at age 88, still living in his old riding of Vancouver Quadra).

The remarkable thing about Green and Diefenbaker is that they are not heroes to the anti-nuclear faction in Canada, having been pioneers in the movement, suffering defeat at the hands of the pro-nuclear Liberals of Lester Pearson because of it.

Green and Diefenbaker confronted the United States

on the issue and earned the undying hatred of President John F. Kennedy, whereas Mulroney seeks closer economic and military ties with the United States, though he emphasizes conventional rather than nuclear capabilities for Canada.

Apart from the hecklers, his pro-American, pro-NATO stands drew the largest cheers of all from his western audiences. Heading East for the final days of the campaign, he left the western battleground to John Turner and Ed Broadbent, confident he would not only hold, but expand, the Tory western bastion that Diefenbaker built, consolidated under Robert Stanfield and Joe Clark. Not bad, he would say, for a kid from Baie Comeau, eh?

Switch to John Turner, who had just come out of a frisky Vancouver TV interview with Jack Webster (boo on Mulroney, snorted the Oatmeal Savage), a leaden-handed audience at the Canadian Club, and an utterly dreadful picnic in his chosen riding.

Boarding the Turner plane, one had to walk past the prime minister in his seat at the front, and our eyes met, and I said it was good to see him, and he said it was good to see me, and neither of us sounded as if we meant it. For him, all the forecasts were bad, including those in Vancouver Quadra.

Hadn't anything nice happened to John Turner during this campaign?

As it turned out, three nice things were to happen to him that very day.

The first nice thing was a breakfast meeting at 7:30 on an Edmonton morning. The Liberal organizers had done their work well, the shopping plaza site was festooned with placards and balloons, and a capacity crowd showed up.

The second nice thing was a luncheon meeting in the concert hall lobby in Saskatoon, where again the advance work had been excellent and people thronged in. Good music, good decor, good spirit.

And the third nice thing was in the Montreal suburb of Pointe Claire, an all-candidates' meeting for the ridings of the largely Anglo end of the island of Montreal, a rip-roaring, old-fashioned political happening, with Turner as the star.

The Liberal leader came to these meetings out of British Columbia, where he had been mistreated at gatherings so badly organized he should have sued his own party for non-support.

In particular, there was a cheerleader named Bill, his last name mercifully lost to posterity, who tried to flog a Chinatown rally and a Croatian picnic into life, when life there was none.

"Here comes the prime minister!" roared Bill. "Hip, hip, hurrah!" No response. "Hip, hip hurrah?" tried Bill. Nothing. "Turner, Tur-ner, Tur-ner" he raved, still solo.

"You're great," he told the 250 people at the Croatian picnic. He should have been throttled, preferably by John Turner's own hands.

In Edmonton, Saskatoon, and Montreal, there were no "Bills," and no need for any. The local Grits came to roar, and roar they did.

Their enthusiasm brought out of Turner the best speeches I had heard from him in the campaign—instead of carrying the crowds on his back, they were putting spirit into him.

That is what partisan crowds are for in election campaigns, and these were partisan crowds, to be sure. The meeting places were too small for the numbers of people who showed up, a practice the politicians have followed ever since 1963 when huge arena rallies in Vancouver for both Diefenbaker and Pearson broke up in disorder.

The meetings did something for Turner when he needed a fix, and that was good to see—not because of pity, but out of sympathy for the man in his predicament. I had seen too many politicians battered, most of them Tories, to feel pity for the Grits in the grinder.

In particular, I had seen what the Liberals themselves did to Joe Clark, when his fellow Tories weren't doing it to him, and I had marvelled at his grace in a pressure cooker that boiled for four years.

And I had vivid recollections of my hero Lester Pearson

suffering the worst political defeat in Canadian history up to then, and hanging onto the remnants of a leadership that seemed to hold no prospects, only to win the prime ministership a scant six years later.

In his disastrous 1958 campaign, Liberal organizers let Pearson down the way they had failed Turner in this election. It might not have mattered, because voters were hell bent for Diefenbaker then, just as they were for Mulroney this time.

Whether John Turner would ever be able to confront those who had failed him, or lied to him, remained to be seen. I certainly didn't begrudge Geills Turner her attacks on those of us she perceived to be her husband's tormentors, though we see ourselves as bearers of truth. And I quite enjoyed the outburst of daughter Elizabeth Turner who said, of media, ''screw 'em all!''

When it was over, John Turner would look back at the campaign and wish that all his days could have been like Tuesday, August 28, with Grits hanging from the chandeliers and everybody chanting his name as if they meant it.

He would know, too, that the day's work netted nothing but a handful of Anglo remnant seats in Montreal, and that in the whole of the West he had only two seats, one of them his own.

The climax of the election campaign was to be Brian Mulroney's speech to the Empire Club in Toronto, at which he had promised to disclose the cost of his campaign promises.

It was a device that had served him well ever since he named the date during the TV debate on women's issues, because it enabled him to sweep the question of costs ahead of him, telling people to wait for it, confident that by August 28 the impression of a Tory landslide would be so vivid it would blot out everything else.

John Turner and Ed Broadbent kept hammering away on Tory costs until even they began to weary of the issue, and of trying to come up with cost figures of their own that would be low enough. Broadbent priced his platform out at a $1.9 billion, and Turner's figures seemed to indicate $4 billion over three years, though it depended on how you held them up to the light.

And Turner came out with a black binder that he said contained 338 of Mulroney's promises, all of which he wanted Mulroney to put prices on in his Toronto speech. Turner, brandishing the binder, looked and sounded uncomfortably like the Senator Joe McCarthy of the 1950s, waving his list of "Commies" and shouting: "I have here in my hand," without ever saying exactly what it was he was brandishing.

"Come clean, Mulroney!" shouted Turner, "tell us how much this catalogue will cost. No fancy footwork."

Reporters who examined the catalogue said it contained everything from detailed promises to general comments about improving relations with the United States.

A covering note from Turner's staff said "every effort has been made to avoid duplication; however, if some doubling up inadvertently has occurred, at least as many other promises likely have been missed."

Turner's "catalogue" evoked memories of another Keith Davey ploy when he was working for Lester Pearson in the elections of the sixties, and sent Liberal "truth squads" on the trail of John Diefenbaker, to the great delight of Dief, who roasted the Grit truth-seekers whenever they appeared.

In politics, as in war, truth is often the first casualty, and voters were not to be much the wiser after Mulroney's revelations, which were less enlightening than his frequent campaign statements that "it's not going to be easy, because when we get in we're going to find an awful mess."

When Mulroney revealed his long-awaited figures, Turner said "the only job he has given Canadians is a snow job." He called the Mulroney speech "a hodge podge of figures," which it certainly was.

The best anybody could make of it was that it came to $4.3 billion over a period of three years, and that there would be further announcements, keeping in mind that all his programs would be spread over the four- or five-year life of his government, and that "nobody would expect everything to be done all at once."

There were, indeed, details—a bewildering array of them defying, as both Turner and Broadbent complained, intelligent analysis, certainly in the days of campaigning that remained.

In the next two years, there would be an additional $400 million for defence, $500 million for youth employment training, $350 million for research and development in the resource and tourist industries, $600 million in social programs, $65 million in transportation, $125 million for forestry rehabilitation, $300 million in mining incentives, $100 million in fishery, $500 million in energy incentives, and $110 million for small business, plus $350 million to stimulate agriculture.

While voters were pondering these figures, Turner put a price tag on his own programs that seemed to total over $5 billion, over three and a half years. His aides argued the total would be pared to $1.6 billion when the effect of spending cuts, a new minimum tax on the rich, and inflation-indexed government bonds, was taken into account.

Lost in the shuffle were the estimates of up to $10 billion that some observers had put on Mulroney's promises, and the forecast in a paper leaked by John Crosbie that the total, over five years, might run to $20 billion.

Said Ed Broadbent: "It raises a very serious question of credibility." Turner said Mulroney was a spinner of deceit, and that it was no wonder the Tories had put a muzzle on Crosbie.

Crosbie himself was in Markham, Ontario, speaking at a rally for North York incumbent John Gamble, a meeting that Mulroney had declined to attend because of his distaste for Gamble's right-wing views. On election day, Gamble's defeat at the hands of independent Tony Roman would be one of the many bright spots for Mulroney.

For the Liberals, it was fitting that the last shots of so wretched an election campaign should be fired by two men who had led the party to its heights, and then cast it into the depths.

Marc Lalonde, Trudeau's alter-ego and finance minister, architect of the National Energy Plan and custodian of the party's fortunes in Quebec, held a press conference to respond to Mulroney's cost estimates.

What he said was that Mulroney was taking the Canadian people for fools, and that the Tory leader had left out 300 of his promises, the total cost of which would be $22 billion.

"Outrageous," said Lalonde with what was to be his final political breath. "There is big, big dough there. There are big, big amounts. Can we trust that man?"

Meanwhile, in Montreal, Pierre Trudeau turned up for an evening of tributes to himself, and the mayor of Cote St. Luc, Bernard Lang, asked the crowd:

"Was he the greatest prime minister we ever had?"

"Yes," came the response.

"Will we ever have another prime minister as great?"

"No!"

And Trudeau said he felt nostalgic, "an emotion by which I am not often touched and to which I never surrender." By now, he was the only smiling Liberal in the land, inscrutable to the last.

Their national campaigns finished, the leaders went to their ridings—Mulroney to Manicouagan, Turner to Vancouver Quadra, Broadbent to Oshawa. The decline of the Liberal Party had been amply chronicled, and the stage was set for the fall, marking 1984 as the longest year for the Grits, and the blackest. Everywhere in the land, and all across Quebec, the political roses had turned blue.

APPENDIX A

ELECTION 1984 RESULTS

Elected

PC	**211**
Lib	**40**
NDP	**30**
Ind	**1**

Percentage of Popular Vote

PC	**50%**
Lib	**28%**
NDP	**18%**
Other	**4%**

Regional Breakdown

Atlantic Region—32 seats

	1984	1980
PC:	25	(13)
Lib:	7	(19)
NDP:	0	(0)
Other:	0	(0)

Quebec—75 seats

	1984	1980
PC:	58	(1)
Lib:	17	(74)
NDP:	0	(0)
Other:	0	(0)

Ontario—95 seats

	1984	1980
PC:	67	(38)
Lib:	14	(52)
NDP:	13	(5)
Other:	1	(0)

Prairies—49 seats

	1984	1980
PC:	39	(33)
Lib:	1	(2)
NDP:	9	(14)
Other:	0	(0)

British Columbia—28 seats

	1984	1980
PC:	19	(16)
Lib:	1	(0)
NDP:	8	(12)
Other:	0	(0)

NWT/Yukon—3 seats

	1984	1980
PC:	3	(2)
Lib:	0	(0)
NDP:	0	(1)
Other:	0	(0)

APPENDIX B

THE NEW PC CABINET

These are the members of the new PC federal cabinet. They are listed in order of precedence, based on the order in which they were appointed:

Brian Mulroney, prime minister
George Hees, veterans affairs
Duff Roblin, Senate government leader
Joe Clark, external affairs
Flora MacDonald, employment and immigration
Erik Nielsen, deputy prime minister, Privy Council
    president
John Crosbie, justice, attorney general
Roch LaSalle, public works
Don Mazankowski, transport
Elmer MacKay, solicitor general
Jake Epp, health and welfare
John Fraser, fisheries and oceans
Sinclair Stevens, regional industrial expansion
John Wise, agriculture
Ray Hnatyshyn, government House leader
David Crombie, Indian affairs and northern development
Robert de Cotret, Treasury Board
Perrin Beatty, national revenue
Michael Wilson, finance
Bob Coates, defence

Jack Murta, multiculturalism
Harvie Andre, supply and services
Otto Jelinek, fitness and amateur sport
Tom Siddon, science and technology
Charles Mayer, wheat board
Bill McKnight, labour
Walter McLean, secretary of state and status of women
Tom McMillan, tourism
Pat Carney, energy, mines and resources
André Bissonnette, small businesses
Suzanne Blais-Grenier, environment
Benoit Bouchard, minister of state for transport
Andrée Champagne, youth
Michel Côté, consumer and corporate affairs
James Kelleher, international trade
Bob Layton, mines
Marcel Masse, communications
Barbara McDougall, minister of state for finance
Gerry Merrithew, forestry
Monique Vézina, external relations

All through the election campaign, Brian Mulroney kept saying that a Grit's idea of heaven was a Senate appointment. He didn't need to add that a Tory's image of paradise was a cabinet post and a crack at the powers and perquisites of the ministry.

So when he won the biggest majority in history, thus obliterating the second of John Diefenbaker's monuments from the record books (the Bill of Rights had already been overridden by Trudeau's Charter), Mulroney hastened to appoint the biggest cabinet ever.

In fact it was a sort of mini-parliament, a cabinet whose sheer numbers approached those of entire legislatures in six of the ten provinces. By delicious design, Mulroney's forty-member cabinet was exactly the same size as the entire Liberal caucus in the House of Commons, rubbing in the fact that the Liberals were left with twice as many senators as MPs.

Mulroney broke his cabinet into nine committees, a

drop from Trudeau's thirteen, and to the key Priorities and
Planning Committee he named eleven veterans of the Joe
Clark cabinet and three newcomers. On the far right was
the new defence minister, Robert Coates, and on the left
was the minister for employment and immigration, Flora
MacDonald. Coates, the supporter of apartheid in South
Africa, and MacDonald the sympathizer with anti-American
revolutions in Central America.

On Coates' side of the spectrum was Sinclair Stevens,
his ambition for the foreign ministry dashed by Joe Clark's
prior claims. Stevens, whose views on foreign affairs had
caused me to liken him to Vlad the Impaler, would channel
his considerable skills and energies into the area of regional
industrial expansion while another portfolio he craved,
finance, went to Michael Wilson.

In the struggle for the Tory leadership, we had seen
Stevens back Mulroney when most of the Tory MPs had
supported Clark. Wilson had chosen to run his own abortive campaign, throwing his support to Mulroney only at the
end. Yet it was to Clark and Wilson that Mulroney awarded
the most prestigious jobs in cabinet, together with Clark
loyalist Erik Nielsen, who was named deputy prime minister.

The cabinet gave further evidence of Mulroney's ge-
nius for compromise and conciliation, enveloping his
former opponents in the party and at the same time rewarding those who had helped him to the top—George
Hees, Elmer MacKay, Stevens and Coates, Jack Murta,
Otto Jelinek, Charles Mayer, Bill McKnight and Walter
McLean. His object was to achieve what had eluded his
predecessors, party unity, and put an end to the eternal
Tory game of "Swallow the Leader."

The prospect of power had kept the Tories together for
more than a year and enabled them to march into battle
under Mulroney's banner, with devastating results for the
Liberals. Once in power, the custom was for the Conservatives to turn their guns on one another—or their knives, to
use Bob Coates' choice of weapons in his book about how
they brought John Diefenbaker down.

The style of the Mulroney government would be set immediately by the man himself, aided by the veterans of the Joe Clark government of 1979. Behind them would be Mulroney's own phalanx of newcomers to high office, most of them newcomers to Parliament itself, including seven French-speaking MPs from Quebec of whom the rest of the country had never heard, picked at random by Mulroney from his new hotshot caucus from French Canada.

Mulroney's French-speaking MPs were twice as numerous as the entire Liberal caucus, and at the Tory victory parties in Ottawa the predominant language seemed to be French. Warm-blooded embraces were more in evidence than the Tory handshakes of old.

Initial public reception of Mulroney's cabinet was favourable, the feeling being that he had struck a nice balance between conflicting elements not only in the party but in the country. Only one critic succumbed to calling it a nuts and bolts cabinet—all the nuts from the Canadian right wing and all the ones who had bolted from Joe Clark to Mulroney.

Mulroney's main problem was that both his caucus and his cabinet were too big, but it was a problem much to be envied by John Turner, who had set a list of records of his own, all of them unenviable. As Jesse Jackson had said in the United States, his grapes had turned to raisins and his joybell had lost its resonance, the only bright spot being that he himself was elected MP for Vancouver Quadra on a last-minute surge of the sympathy vote.

Turner was left to contemplate the wreckage of the Liberal Party and to hope he could emulate Lester Pearson, who found himself in a similar predicament in 1958. The difference, though, was that this time the Conservatives had a manager in charge, a man who had engineered a series of political miracles, aided by the departure of Pierre Trudeau and general public weariness with Grits in office.

I myself had prayed to God that he would, just once before I quit, let me cover something other than a Liberal government in power in Ottawa. And after the votes were counted on September 4, I cast my eyes upward once more and said: "Thank you, God, but you went too far!"